MEANWHILE, IN RUSSIA

T0286714

Russian Shorts

Russian Shorts is a series of thought-provoking books published in a slim format. The Shorts books examine key concepts, personalities, and moments in Russian historical and cultural studies, encompassing its vast diversity from the origins of the Kievan state to Putin's Russia. Each book is intended for a broad range of readers, covers a side of Russian history and culture that has not been well-understood, and is meant to stimulate conversation.

Willard Sunderland, Henry R. Winkler Professor of Modern History, University of Cincinnati, USA

Published Titles

Pussy Riot: Speaking Punk to Power, Eliot Borenstein
Memory Politics and the Russian Civil War: Reds Versus Whites, Marlene Laruelle and Margarita Karnysheva
Russian Utopia: A Century of Revolutionary Possibilities, Mark Steinberg
Racism in Modern Russia, Eugene M. Avrutin
Meanwhile, In Russia: Russian Internet Memes and Viral Video, Eliot Borenstein
The Afterlife of the 'Soviet Man': Rethinking Homo Sovieticus, Gulnaz Sharafutdinova

Upcoming Titles

Art, History and the Making of Russian National Identity: Vasily Surkiov, Viktor Vasnetsov, and the Remaking of the Past, Stephen M. Norris
Russia and the Jewish Question: A Modern History, Robert Weinberg
The Soviet Gulag: History and Memory, Jeffrey S. Hardy
The Multiethnic Soviet Union and its Demise, Brigid O'Keeffe
Russian Food since 1800: Empire at Table, Catriona Kelly
A Social History of the Russian Army, Roger R. Reese
Why We Need Russian Literature, Angela Brintlinger
Nuclear Russia, Paul Josephson

MEANWHILE, IN RUSSIA

RUSSIAN INTERNET MEMES
AND VIRAL VIDEO

Eliot Borenstein

BLOOMSBURY ACADEMIC
LONDON • NEW YORK • OXFORD • NEW DELHI • SYDNEY

BLOOMSBURY ACADEMIC
Bloomsbury Publishing Plc
50 Bedford Square, London, WC1B 3DP, UK
1385 Broadway, New York, NY 10018, USA
29 Earlsfort Terrace, Dublin 2, Ireland

BLOOMSBURY, BLOOMSBURY ACADEMIC and the Diana logo are
trademarks of Bloomsbury Publishing Plc

First published in Great Britain 2022

Series design by Tjaša Krivec
Sculpture by Margriet van Breevoort
Photo by Alexander Dhiet

A catalogue record for this book is available from the British Library.

Library of Congress Cataloging-in-Publication Data

Names: Borenstein, Eliot, 1966- author.
Title: Meanwhile, in Russia: Russian internet memes and viral video / Eliot Borenstein.
Description: 1 Edition. | New York, NY : Bloomsbury Academic, 2022. |
Series: Russian shorts | Includes bibliographical references and index.
Identifiers: LCCN 2021036305 (print) | LCCN 2021036306 (ebook) |
ISBN 9781350181526 (paperback) | ISBN 9781350181533 (hardback) |
ISBN 9781350181557 (pdf) | ISBN 9781350181540 (ebook)
Subjects: LCSH: Memes–Russia (Federation) | Digital media–Political aspects–
Russia (Federation) | Internet and activism–Russia (Federation) |
Politics and culture–Russia (Federation)
Classification: LCC HM626 .B67 2022 (print) | LCC HM626 (ebook) |
DDC 384.3/80947–dc23
LC record available at https://lccn.loc.gov/2021036305
LC ebook record available at https://lccn.loc.gov/2021036306

ISBN: PB: 978-1-3501-8152-6
HB: 978-1-3501-8153-3
ePDF: 978-1-3501-8155-7
eBook: 978-1-3501-8154-0

Typeset by Deanta Global Publishing Services, Chennai, India
Printed and bound in India

To find out more about our authors and books visit www.bloomsbury.com
and sign up for our newsletters.

For Lev Bernstein,

Who knows his memes

CONTENTS

FIGURES

ACKNOWLEDGMENTS

This is probably the most crowdsourced book I will ever write. I solicited meme suggestions on Facebook, received random memes from friends by email, and benefited greatly from the audience for my online lectures. When it comes to source material, there are too many people for me to count, let alone remember by name. So instead, please imagine that I have sent you a cat meme expressing my thanks.

In addition to this general expression of gratitude, there are a few people, groups, and organizations that must be mentioned. First, the Jordan Center for the Advanced Study of Russia at NYU. Joshua Tucker, the center's director, has been supportive of this project from the beginning and helped me refine the idea for what became a seventeen-part online lecture series to keep a sense of community going during the spring 2020 Covid-19 lockdown. That series, "Russian Internet Memes: The Short Course," gave me the opportunity to workshop many of the chapters of the present book, as well as explore avenues that could not be included for lack of space.[1] Alexandra Shpitalnik, the Jordan Center's Program Administrator, made the whole thing technically possible (in addition to having some meme suggestions of her own). The lecture series was, for me, more than just a chance to share my research; each week, I got to see friendly faces (anywhere from 30 to 100) and remind myself that I'm not alone. Again, my thanks to everyone who attended.

Portions of this book appeared in different form on my blog, *Russia's Alien Nations* (cross-posted with the *All the Russias* blog at the Jordan Center, thanks to Maya Vinokour). In addition, I have reused some material from my article "Survival of the Catchiest: Memes and Postmodernism in Russia" (*Slavic and East European Journal* 48.3 (2004): 462–84 for Chapter 1, from "Borders Unpatrolled: Imaginary Geographies and the Spaces of Performance in Russian Viral

Acknowledgments

Video." (Buckler, Julie, Julie Cassiday, and Boris Wolfson. *Russian Performances*. Madison: University of Wisconsin Press, 2018: 139–47 for Chapter 6), and from "Post-Soviet Masculinities and the Vanishing Subject." *The Routledge International Handbook to Gender in Central-Eastern Europe and Eurasia* (Katalin Fabiran, Janet E. Johnson, and Mara Lazda, eds.).

As always, I am grateful to my family. To Fran for being patient with all the ridiculous memes I showed her; to Louis, for being a walking Internet meme in his own right, and especially to Lev, who speaks the language of memes like a native. If I have avoided looking old and out of touch, it is all thanks to him.

A NOTE ON RESOURCES

All the memes and viral videos referenced in *Meanwhile, in Russia* can be found on my website, eliotborenstein.net, along with links to where I originally found them.

INTRODUCTION
IVAN THE TERRIBLE KILLS EVERYBODY

To the delight of millions, Ivan the Terrible has been making a comeback. His revival has also been a return to form: the merciless tsar is leaving a trail of bodies in his wake in a vivid demonstration that he hasn't lost his knack for bloodletting. After famously killing his own son, as depicted in Ilya Repin's 1885 painting showing him cradling the young man's bloody corpse, Ivan has, since 2013, murdered Jean-Paul Marat, R2D2, the Chrysler Building, Lenin, Kenny from *South Park*, Munch's *The Scream*, and even Kazimir Malevich's infamous black square. Dead for over four centuries, he shows no signs of slowing down.[1]

Ivan owes his afterlife to a popular Internet meme whose collected variations go by the name "Ivan the Terrible Kills Everybody" («Иван Грозный убивает всех»). Only some of these memes replace his son with a new victim; in others, the image of Ivan and his son appears in unlikely settings, such as inside an elevator as part of a fake public service announcement about the dangers of rapidly closing doors. Sometimes his deployment is political, such as when he is photoshopped into images of street protests. After all, one expects a political subtext whenever this notorious tsar is invoked, as in Mikhail Bulgakov's 1934–6 play *Ivan Vasilievich*, which magically transports the despot to Stalinist Moscow (or Leonid Gaidai's subsequent 1973 film version, which brings him into the much less bloodthirsty Brezhnev era).[2] But most of the time, the juxtaposition of Ivan is simply absurd, with absurdity being the point. Ivan the Terrible, first of the tsars, conqueror of Siberia and author of Russia's first reign of terror may just be there for the lulz.[3]

Yet it turns out that even absurdity can have a political impact. Repin's painting has been controversial since it was first unveiled, but the meme only began in 2013. That same year, a group of historians and activists wrote a letter to Russian culture minister Vladimir Medinsky demanding that "Ivan the Terrible and His Son" be removed from the Tretyakov Gallery, since its very existence is slanderous to the tsar's memory (they claim that no such murder took place) (Coal).[4] Whatever one might think of the credentials or judgment of the letters' signatories, they were clearly unprepared for the world of the Internet. Repin's painting became an example of the Streisand Effect, when the demand for suppression or privacy leads to the proliferation of the very image the petitioner hopes not to spread. The result was "Ivan the Terrible Kills Everybody."

There is much to be learned from this story, but only as part of a larger investigation of the evolution of culture on the Russian Internet.[5] Though the Internet began making significant inroads into the Russian Federation throughout the 1990s, the growth of a truly immersive online culture largely coincides with the era of Vladimir Putin. Refreshingly, this is not another story of Russia "lagging behind" the West; developments in twenty-first-century Internet and New Media cultures happened at roughly the same pace in Russia as in the rest of Europe. They did not, however, arise under the same conditions.

Taking its name from a popular Russian-themed site, *Meanwhile, in Russia* examines the rise of Internet memes and viral video on the Russian-language Internet (commonly called the "Runet"), as well as investigating what happens when this material crosses over into the Anglophone world.

Mixed Messages

Memes and viral video on the Russian Internet could have—and have—easily been the subject of books at least twice as long as this one. The scholarship on Internet memes has been growing at an impressive pace (not by Internet standards, of course, but academic publishing is a dial-up modem compared to the high speeds that meme-makers take for granted), while the Russian Internet's history and architecture still await a definitive study. Russian online video began in its own universe parallel to YouTube, the portal that now hosts most of its content, but in many ways, it is still very much a world apart. A short book could not even catalog the major examples of Russian Internet memes and viral video, let alone provide a critical analysis, and in any case, an attempt at a real-time map of Russian online participatory culture would be outdated by the time the book was published.

What this book aims to do is more modest in some regards and more ambitious in others. While the English language and Latin alphabet are still dominant in the online world, they are not unchallenged. China is an obvious example of an Internet culture that, while intersecting with English-language sites, has its own language and its own political and economic parameters. On a somewhat smaller scale, the same can be said for Russia. As a former superpower and current cultural, political, and economic force to be reckoned with, Russia is a fascinating case study of a mostly non-English Internet culture that is both globally connected and locally rooted. By the same token, the concerns this book addresses are a similar combination of the global and the local.

Internet memes and viral video did not originate in Russia, but they have become thoroughly rooted in the Russian-speaking world's media ecosystem.[6] That ecosystem has its own conditions and pressures, as well as its own history, all of which are dealt with in Chapter 2. Certainly, politics plays an important role, and memes and videos with an explicit political orientation are treated in Chapter 5. In a country with a long history of censorship and state overreach, the Internet in general and viral content in particular have provided a relatively safe space for satire, dissent, and downright mockery of those who hold the levers of power.

Indeed, it is the political aspect of Russian memes and viral video that have received the bulk of Western scholarly attention, particularly in relation to the war in Ukraine and Russia's seizure of Crimea.[7] Anastasia Denisova's 2019 excellent comparative study *Internet Memes and Society: Social, Cultural, and Political Contexts* features several chapters with acute analysis of Russian Internet memes, but the book's subtitle also makes its focus clear: while Denisova by no means ignores the frivolous and playful, politics are at the forefront.[8] There is every reason to emphasize politics, but for the present, much shorter study, I want to make sure that readers come away with an understanding that the Russian Internet, like Russia itself, is about more than politics, and perhaps not even primarily politics. Russian online discourse is every bit as insane, hilarious, offensive, and pointless as anything that can be found in English.

But I must also make an immediate counterpoint: Russian memes and viral video may not primarily be concerned with Politics with a capital "P," but it would be naive to forget that there is nothing cultural that is entirely outside of or immune to politics writ large. In the various battles between the proponents of a free Internet and representatives of the state, conflict is as likely to arise over questions of "morality" and "appropriateness" as they are of explicit government policy. As we shall see in the discussions of the moral panics surrounding twerking videos in Chapter 7, the state critics inevitably resemble the stodgy defenders of the status quo in a formulaic Hollywood movie, completely outmatched by the playfulness and unbridled energy of their insouciant opponents. In my imaginary movie, those same critics would inevitably be (literally) swayed by the power of art in the film's closing act, even dancing awkwardly as the credits roll. But life does not always imitate (bad) art.

Indeed, it is the reflexive insouciance of the online world that may well be the greatest ongoing challenge to Russian officialdom. The state media and United Russia party officials are typically prone to a level of self-seriousness that could almost be self-parody, and they are at a loss when confronted with absurdity. The refusal to engage with official discourse on its own terms is a common thread running through Internet culture, the 2012–14 protest movement, and the anarchist punk feminist music of Pussy Riot.

This commonality points to one of the main concerns of the present book. Discussing Internet memes and viral video, or online culture in general, as an entirely self-contained sphere makes less and less sense as time goes on. Partitioning the Internet from the "real world" does justice to neither. It is not a binary proposition; even the "always online" are simultaneously off-line. As the next chapter will show, the very term "meme" was not initially connected to the Internet and has a scope and import that encompasses all aspects of culture and communication. Just as the idea of the meme migrated to the Internet, Internet memes themselves typically circulate in a framework that includes the off-line world. Throughout this book, I will emphasize the larger informational ecosystem of Internet memes and viral video, suggesting that we reexamine our understanding of the online/off-line dynamic.

Meanwhile, in Russia pays particular attention to the construction of Russia and Russian identity in viral content. Coming to conclusions about the lived experience or "essence" of a culture based on media, film, and fiction is a dubious proposition: there will always be significant gaps between representation and reality. But reality is not, strictly speaking, the subject of this book: media and cultural production extend or complement our individual understanding of the word, representing places and experiences that are not readily available to us. But they also subtly shape our understanding even of things we do experience directly, providing a narrative framework for ordering the events unfolding around us.

This is true everywhere there are media, but with particular resonance for Russia. The upheavals connected to the dismantling of the Soviet Union, the economic displacement, traumatic loss of great-power status, and ideological vacuum left by the collapse of the Communist Party provoked a great deal of soul searching and even more verbiage, with calls for a rearticulation of the "Russian Idea" (a spiritual/ideological mission statement for the country). The idea of the Russian idea was formulated by the émigré philosopher Nikolai Berdyaev in 1946, and it is perhaps the passage of time that has made attempts to revive it so futile. Russianness is contested in other arenas: film, fiction, music, and pop culture.[9] And recently, it has begun to be negotiated in the viral content on the Internet.

Russian memes and viral video hold a mirror up to Russia for (self-)reflection, but they are also among the country's most visible cultural exports. Long a powerhouse in the world of high culture (Tchaikovsky, Dostoevsky, Malevich), Russia has been less successful in making its own mark on mass culture. Besides Pussy Riot, whose success is more a matter of politics than aesthetics, Russia as a producer of pop culture is nearly invisible on the world stage. The girl band t.A.T.u. gained notoriety for its fake lesbianism but quickly vanished from the popular consciousness. The only truly great success story has been the animated series *Masha and the Bear*, a runaway hit on Netflix. But memes are another matter. The Internet cannot get enough of images and videos about perceived Russian excess: like it or not, drunken fights, squatting Slavs, and road rage are Russia's virtual calling card. How this all plays out is the subject of Chapter 6.

The book ends with a chapter that was not part of the original plan. Like everything else in the world, work on this project was turned upside down by Covid-19. The uncomfortable truth is that a global pandemic that cost over three million lives, destroyed the world economy, and facilitated new heights of authoritarianism on the part of leaders just looking for an excuse to crack down inevitably sparked an explosion of Internet memes. Among the many inventive trends in Russian memetic content was the creation of the "Izoizoliatsiia" ("Isolation Art") group on Facebook, in which Russians reenacted famous paintings while sheltered in place. But the term "Isolation" also proved ironic, since this particular group drew attention to Russian Internet culture from around the world. The first months of the pandemic were also an opportunity to watch coronavirus memes cross linguistic and national borders, circulating globally even as a huge portion of the world's population was stuck at home. As I will explain in Chapter 1, I have qualms about the adoption of the "viral" metaphor for memes. But in this case, at least, the metaphor is hard to resist.

Methodology (and the Fight against It)

Among the many catchy formulations to be found in the Russian language is one that became quite common in Soviet times and remains current today: "X and the fight against it." This highly productive (non-Internet) meme is a way of announcing a topic while immediately framing it in terms of opposition: "Alcoholism and the Fight against It," for instance.

I have borrowed this meme (without asking for the Russian language's permission) not to declare all-out war on methodology, or even to make the naive claim that it is possible to work with no methodology whatsoever. My intent is simply to warn the reader not to expect this short book to fit within the framework of the social sciences. As new and digital phenomena, Internet memes can be comfortably assimilated as data, and one could reasonably expect charts and graphs about the frequency, popularity, and decline of various Internet memes over time, as well as a comparative analysis of their various sources. None of this can be found in the present volume.

I am not trained as a social scientist and cannot pretend to have any real interest in the compilation of empirical data, nor can I hide my intermittent skepticism about the results. More to the point, were I to attempt such an approach, it would be misleading and dishonest, since it is not within my skill set.

Instead, I treat Internet memes the same way I approach the materials I have been studying for decades, namely literature, film, television, advertisements, religious brochures, and pornography. It is all information, but the meanings are to be teased out (if not created) discursively through analyzing content and context while avoiding claims that these materials accurately represent actual, lived experience.

The memes and videos discussed in this book were found in the simplest possible manner: through search engines (Google, Yandex), social media (Facebook, Twitter, VKontakte, Telegram, Instagram), traditional media, and personal recommendations. While this could be called lazy, I would argue that laziness is the point. With the exception of some particularly niche content on certain VKontakte groups, these are the memes that are easy for casual Internet users to find. Most of them are always merely a click or two away, which means they are accessible parts of the Russian Internet landscape.

To make things easier on the reader, I have reduced this small number of clicks even further. In addition to the images reproduced in this book, all of these memes and videos are available on my website, eliotborenstein.net, which also contains information about their sourcing. Feel free to send me more memes, and I may add them to the collection.

CHAPTER 1
GETTING MEMES WRONG

___

Ye Olde Memes

When I was a boy in the days before the Internet, memes had to walk uphill both ways, barefoot in the snow, to get anybody's attention.

Obviously, this is not true, and it's not even a particularly elegant metaphor. But it is an example of a meme ("When I was your age, I had to walk to school") given a change in form and context, as often happens with memes. It is a meme, but not an Internet meme. If it gets replicated in multiple copies of the present book and read by more than a handful of people, then it will be a relatively successful meme about the relationship between Internet memes and memes in general. It will only become an Internet meme if people find it amusing and start sharing it online, the odds of which are slim to none.

Most of the time, when people refer to memes, they specifically mean Internet memes. This is an example of semantic drift, the tendency for some terms to accrue new, unexpected meanings over time. For scholars of memetics (the "science" of memes), this is both frustrating, in that the original meaning of the word is obscured, and gratifying, in that the very fact of the word's mutation can be cited as proof that meme theory is valid. By the end of this chapter, that last sentence should make sense. Please be sure to come back here and check.

The Descent of Memes

The term "meme" was coined by Richard Dawkins, probably more famous to younger readers either for his militant atheism or for Matt

Stone and Trey Parker's hilarious R-rated parody of him in a pair of 2006 episodes of *South Park*.[1] Dawkins is an evolutionary biologist whose 1976 book, *The Selfish Gene*, was a radical reconception of Darwinism, with memes proposed almost as an afterthought.

Dawkins's thesis was simple and revolutionary: the true subject, or hero, of evolution is not the organism or species but the genes that the organism passes along from generation to generation. This "genes-eye view" sees the organism as "survival mechanism" for the genes it carries. To explain this, Dawkins proposes the categories of "vehicles" and "replicators." "Replicators" are the things that are actually subject to natural selection, making multiple copies of themselves whose fidelity is not guaranteed: most of the copies will look like the original, but some will have a random mutation. If that mutation provides an advantage, the mutated version may eventually crowd out the original. He writes, "DNA molecules are replicators. They generally . . . gang together into large communal survival machines or 'vehicles.'"[2]

Over the course of his work beyond *The Selfish Gene*, Dawkins makes clear that he is arguing for a phenomenon he calls "Universal Darwinism," which proposes that in any system with scarce resources, replication, and an imperfect copying mechanism, the result will resemble Darwinian biological evolution. At the end of *The Selfish Gene*, he is already arguing for an application of Darwinism to other replicators. His case in point is the meme, a term he himself has coined. A meme is a basic unit of culture.

Applying Darwinism to culture has a long and unsavory history, thanks in no small part to Social Darwinism, an egregious recasting of bigotry as science in order to reinforce then-current preconceptions about racial hierarchies. Even if we ignore the heavy shadow this long-discredited movement still casts, there is also the problem of overly "biologizing" culture by assuming that every facet of human society, interaction, and creativity stems from some hidden biological drive (which, once again, often involves assuming one's own biases or time-bound traditions are "natural" or "primal" rather than contingent). In proposing the meme, however, Dawkins already has an answer to his critics. He is not assuming that culture is biological; rather, he is assuming that culture evolves according to the same system of replication and competition seen in biology. He writes:

> For more than three thousand million years, DNA has been the only replicator worth talking about in the world. But it does not necessarily hold these monopoly rights for all time. Whenever conditions arise in which a new kind of replicator can make copies of itself, the new replicators will tend to take over, and start a new kind of evolution of their own. Once this new evolution begins, it will in no necessary sense be subservient to the old. The old gene-selected evolution, by making brains, provided the soup in which the first memes arose. Once self-copying memes had arisen, their own, much faster, kind of evolution took off. We biologists have assimilated the idea of genetic evolution so deeply that we tend to forget that it is only one of many possible kinds of evolution.[3]

In proposing the meme, Dawkins posits a Darwinian process that is almost entirely divorced from biology. The sole concession to biological determinism is his hypothesis that human beings have a genetic drive toward copying or imitation. This drive essentially kickstarts the process of memetic evolution. By analogy to genes, memes are the smallest, most basic information of culture. Like genes, they initially depend on living organisms as vehicles for survival. If I hum a tune, and you hear, and then you hum it back to me, that is the successful replication of a meme (the tune).

If we accept the concept of memes (a big "if," but let's go along with it), then memes were replicated on a face-to-face level (or, as memeticists would have it, "brain to brain") long before humans developed the means to preserve their culture in other forms. With the development of the visual arts and writing, memes gained access to new vehicles with lifespans potentially much longer than that of the average human.

The ability of memes to be stored and transmitted in the absence of direct human contact is key here, as it is connected to a fundamental question about memes themselves: Why do some memes survive while others do not? Most memes are replicated because they grab someone's attention; as I have indicated elsewhere, memetic selection is not the survival of the fittest but survival of the catchiest.[4] In the absence of other external social or cultural factors, memes must be memorable to be reproduced. Just four years after Dawkins coined the term "meme," Charles J. Lumsden and E. O. Wilson proposed that the basic unit in their evolutionary model of culture be called the "culturegen."[5] The culturegen is basically the same thing as the meme, but with one salient difference: far from catchy, the word is downright clunky.[6] For the term to survive, the evolutionary model that it anchors would have to be so compelling as to outweigh the clumsiness of the word. "Meme," however, is simple and easy to say; it has saturated the culture. "Culturegen" is a historical curiosity, known only to specialists (and now to my readers, who I imagine will quickly forget it). Compared to "culturegen," "meme" is simply a much better meme.

Fortunately for many memes, catchiness is not the sole survival strategy. If a culture or society values a particular set of memes highly, they will be transmitted through institutional power, such as schools and churches. Institutional support of memes is greatly facilitated by the invention of long-term storage media, such as books, and eventually, audio and video recording. Generations of American schoolchildren could have been expected to read at least one of the following works: *The Scarlet Letter, The Great Gatsby,* a Shakespeare play, *The Outsiders,* and possibly something by Hemingway or Steinbeck. Some of these children fell in love with some of these texts, went to graduate school, and wrote scholarly books on obscure topics (Russian Internet memes, for instance). But most of them slogged through their assigned reading, becoming unwilling vehicles for memes whose survival was ensured by canonization rather than catchiness.

As a scientific endeavor, memetics did not initially show a great deal of catchiness, and it certainly was not headed toward canonization. Many scholars in the various disciplines on which memetics impinged (psychology, communications, linguistics, evolutionary biology, to name a few) found the entire endeavor to be rather shaky. One very valid criticism of meme theory is that the definition of the meme is vague, and that no one can prove that memes actually exist.[7] Memeticists respond that Darwinian evolution was developed before the gene itself was discovered; just because we cannot isolate the meme doesn't mean it does not exist.[8]

That may be true, but even this defense reminds us of one of memetics' greatest weaknesses: it seems to rely more on metaphor and analogy than empirical evidence. I would personally not stake my reputation on a full-throated defense of meme theory as a science, but that is because I have no need for it to be scientifically true in order for it to be useful. Its use value is largely a matter of perspective, in that, once you start to see how memes (allegedly) operate, you can pay attention to the aspects of cultural development, interaction, and communication that you might otherwise miss. Meme theory is a useful set of lenses through which to look at the world; if these lenses prove to be nothing more than augmented reality, they may still have something of value to show us.

The Internet, or the Home Memes Never Knew They Had Been Looking for All Along

Whether or not memes truly are the building block of culture, why did it take until 1976 for them to be "discovered"? And why did the idea eventually catch on? It helped that geneticists, like quantum physicists, were inclined to reconsider their subject matter (biological heredity and physical reality, respectively) in terms of *information*, a flexible and fungible category that favors the recognition of commonalities among seemingly disparate phenomena (again, biology and physics). But it also helped that the world was embarking on the second phase of an information revolution.

Before the first half of the twentieth century was over, virtually all forms of cultural expression could now be stored and preserved through some sort of recording mechanism; the next half-century saw the proliferation of means by which these recordings could be transmitted. When *The Selfish Gene* came out, computers were still a mysterious and vaguely sinister novelty in the eyes of nonspecialists. ARPANET, the US Defense Department's computer network, was just seven years away from the adoption of the Transmission Control

Protocol and Internet Protocol (TCP/IP) that enabled the creation of the Internet as we now know it. Long before it became the primary vehicle for distributing music and video, the Internet slowly taught users that words (arguably our primary form of information) could be understood entirely separate from their storage media.[9] Meme theory had been around since 1976, but it took the Internet for memes to start making intuitive sense.

In the October 1994 issue of *Wired* magazine, Mike Godwin wrote a brief article commonly cited as the birthplace of the "Internet meme," although technically, Godwin does not use (or coin) the actual term: in "Meme, Counter-Meme," he discusses what is now called "Godwin's Law," which he first proposed in a Usenet group: "As an online discussion grows longer, the probability of a comparison involving Hitler approaches 1."[10] Godwin's Law is often referred to as the first Internet meme although one could also argue that his article is the source the first Internet meta-meme: the meme of the Internet meme itself. In any case, it is not long after "Meme, Counter-Meme" that "Internet memes" started to be a commonly recognized phenomenon.

Over the course of this book, we will repeatedly see that the Internet meme does not exist in a vacuum; some of the most successful Internet memes have an origin, second life, or both, that is off-line. The success of the Internet meme concept also owes a great deal to off-line discourse. In particular, memetic transmission over computer networks was popularized in the 1980s and 1990s in the first literary movement to explore the ramifications of a networked world in which information is key: the science fiction subgenre known as cyberpunk. Cyberpunk writers did not often use the term "meme" per se, instead focusing on a framing of the meme that has had the greatest memetic success: the idea of the viral.

Though we are all familiar with the term now, the "viral" concept remains controversial in memetics circles. It was popularized (i.e., made into a memetic success) by Richard Brodie, a computer programmer who, after creating Microsoft Word, went on to become a motivational speaker and professional poker player. His 1995 book, *Virus of the Mind: The New Science of the Meme*, was predicated on a metaphor that made memes look like foreign invaders.[11]

14

The viral metaphor is attractive for discussions of persuasion, propaganda, and influence, but it is symptomatic of a naive approach to human psychology, not to mention memes. The assumption seems to be that we are all independent, self-contained subjects whose mental existence that can be somehow conceived of in a vacuum. If this mind chooses to interact with other minds, it may or may not accept information offered to it, but it is ultimately sovereign and independent. Yet philosophers for over a century have called into question the idea of the autonomous human subject, going as far as seeing the self as an illusion emerging from the interactive processes in which the mind engages.

Framing memes as a virus also introduces a false distinction: if memes exist, then they exist both within the mind and as influences coming from without. There is no difference between a "viral" meme and a nonviral meme other than degrees of success. And not only does the viral metaphor conjure up images of a mind under siege, but it also renders the individual subject far too passive. Henry Jenkins and his collaborators prefer to speak of "spreadable" rather than "viral" media, emphasizing the role of individual and group agency in the participatory culture of postmodern media.[12]

"Viral" is now a term associated with marketing strategies (i.e., persuasion), but it is even more commonly applied to video clips that users share quickly and widely. One could distinguish the "viral" video from memetic phenomena, because videos, unlike memes, tend to be shared in perfect, unaltered digital copies. Yet, the most successful viral videos spawn tributes, imitations, parodies, and remixes. In other words, viral videos are another kind of meme.

This book considers Internet memes and viral videos together in that they are both memetic phenomena that thrive on the Internet, point to an off-line world, and create interpretive communities (people who get the joke). There will be many times when distinguishing between the two will be important, due largely to issues of form. But they play similar roles in the construction of national identities on the Internet, for both foreign and domestic consumption.

CHAPTER 2
THE SOVIET MEMETIC LANDSCAPE

In the West, Internet memes were the latest manifestation of an information-saturated environment, preceded by decades of increasingly short nuggets of video content viewed primarily on television (particularly commercials and music videos). But in the former Soviet Union (and, presumably, Eastern Europe, though this is beyond the scope of the present study), the fast pace of the mass media was still quite recent. Soviet television was a slow and soporific affair by the standards of American prime time, almost as if it had been designed as a nature preserve for an endangered species of talking heads. One would never guess from the editing of televised content that this was the country that had pioneered the montage technique. Meanwhile, print was strictly controlled, with even typewriters registered by the government.

Famous for its centrally controlled economy (starting with Stalin's First Five-Year Plan in 1928), the Soviet Union's leadership and bureaucracy set great store by the central oversight of information. At its height under Stalin, the apparatus of the Soviet state poured money, time, and resources into the proliferation of propaganda—a term that, in Russian, was neutral and might be considered analogous to "public relations." Looked at through the lens of memetics, the Soviet Union was an immense factory dedicated to the fabrication and distribution of persuasive memes. As early as the 1920s, a time of relative freedom of expression before Stalin's consolidation of power, Bolshevik activists used the power of the printing press (and, eventually, the radio) to mobilize support among the population and educate them about Leninist theory and Soviet policy. The futurist poet and artist Vladimir Mayakovsky famously lent his talent to the creation of arresting images and catchy slogans, all in the implicit recognition of what the social media age has made obvious: the masses' attention is a limited resource that must be cultivated.[1] For the attention economy, the unprecedented success of the Soviet campaign to end illiteracy was tantamount to a grand infrastructure process that brought the memes of state socialism directly to their target audience (the people).

Early Soviet propaganda posters and slogans were relatively catchy and inventive. Combining the influences of the Russian icon and the futurist avant-garde, the posters often featured dynamic figures on the move, clever layouts and composition, and compelling visual metaphors. Take, for example, "Down with Kitchen Slavery!" (1931). In the bottom corner, a woman stands with her arms elbow deep in water, cleaning her family's clothes. We only see her from the back, but standing in front of her is a woman dressed all in red (of course), opening a large window that is somehow askew from the apartment. Outside is a brand new building with a cafeteria and the words "new lifestyle" printed across them. The woman in red is showing her benighted sister the way to freedom.

Even more than Stalin's Five-Year Plans, the desperate struggle of the Second World War–inspired propagandists to ever-more inventive appeals, such as the world-famous "The Motherland Is Calling" (1941), in which a stern, red-clad Mother Russia raises her left hand high, while her right displays the military oath, her body framed by an array of bayonets. Or her male counterpart from the Russian Civil War, the Red Army man holding a rifle in his left hand as he points to the view with his right: "Have you signed up?" (1920)

After the war, the propaganda campaigns gradually lost all semblances of originality, recycling images and artistic styles that had long gone stale. The slogans were so predictable they could have been generated by algorithm ("We will fulfill the decisions of the nth Congress of the Communist Party of the Soviet Union!"). Little about them demanded attention, which meant they could be both ubiquitous and functionally invisible. The Soviet Union of 1984 bore little resemblance to the Oceania of Orwell's *1984*; compared to the advertising-saturated capitalist West, it was a memetic isolation chamber, with few attention-grabbing words and images capable of overcoming the sheer monotony that inadvertently shielded its citizens from intrusive messaging.

Still, the Soviet city had avenues for messaging that were different from what was customary in the West. Politically themed murals on walls occupied a space somewhat similar to advertising billboards, as did the slogans plastered throughout public transportation. But Soviet public space, from outdoor parks to school to places of work, also had *stengazety* ("Wall newspapers") where a bored passerby could read without purchasing any printed material.[2] Moreover, not all these *stengazety* were simply copies of readily available periodicals; local schools and enterprises produced *stengazety* of their own. Public space was the informational habitat for exhortation and information, however, easily tuned out. The memetic strategy was based on ubiquity and the absence of competition rather than on catchiness and appeal.

Late Socialism also had another avenue for memetic dissemination that significantly differed from anything found in the West: a thriving urban folk culture, manifested primarily in the highly developed joke (anecdote) culture that mocked official propaganda while also turning historical figures and heroes of Soviet film into the protagonists of satirical or absurd humorous stories.[3] Of course, such jokes constitute memes or complexes of memes in the strict sense developed by Dawkins; these were pieces of information that spread from speaker to speaker, mutating into new forms thanks to errors in reproduction.

But they also functioned like Internet memes before the Internet: they were catchy, humorous, and subversive pieces of information that practically begged to be shared and adapted. The mere presence of such folk heroes as Vovka the scamp, Chapaev the famous military commander, Stirlitz the Second World War spy, and Rabinovich the Jew sets the tone for the jokes in which they starred. There was even a joke that perfectly encapsulated the extent to which such jokes had colonized the popular consciousness: two men reduce each other to helpless laughter not by actually telling jokes, but by referring to famous anecdotes by their number ("Number 5!" "Number 12!") Finally, one of them calls out "Number 27!" and the other man scolds him: "Not with ladies present!"

Most Internet memes can be considered a subset of folk culture, but this is an insight that is obscured by their status as pixels rather thanks actual speech. The Russian context makes this connection clearer by virtue of the brief time span between the heyday of oral folk genres (the 1980s) and the Internet folklore constituted by memes (the early twenty-first century). The bridge connecting the two phenomena is post-Soviet television and the replacement of state persuasion methods with capitalist (or at least market-oriented) technologies.

This process began with the advent of Perestroika (1986–91) when censorship was relaxed, political debate encouraged, and new approaches to artistic production and entertainment could find popular venues. Posters, slogans, and the news itself grew far more interesting but would prove no match for the subsequent flood of Western and domestic advertising, along with the adoption of faster-paced television formats, often of a much shorter duration.

Advertising was an attention-grabbing novelty when it took off in the last years of the Soviet Union. In an economy where private industry and commerce were (officially) nonexistent and consumer goods were often in short supply, Soviet viewers had been spared the endless barrage of commercial advertisements that were a fixture of the American television landscape. The last thing the Soviet economy needed was the creation of more demand. Nonetheless, commercial advertisements did exist, thanks to a Brezhnev-era reorientation toward consumer goods and the concomitant need to learn about and affect the internal market.[4] From 1967 to 1991, one Estonian company was allegedly responsible for producing the entirety of the USSR's 5,000–6,000 commercials.[5] This was a huge number for a single company but, by Western standards, minuscule for a country the size of the Soviet Union over twenty-four years.

For the most part, these were commercials for products that did not exist; and if they did exist, they were not widely available. The website for Retro Soviet Ads, which hosts a compilation of some of the surviving clips, put it well: "The Soviet ads simply ignored the idea of selling a product or targeting certain consumers, thus making the ads themselves the product to be consumed."[6] They were the Platonic ideal of the commercial; some of the most successful ads in the history of television give almost no information about the product, so why not dispense with the product altogether? These ads functioned as a kind of state-sanctioned conceptual art and have gained a new audience online thanks to their sheer strangeness. The "Kana" minced chicken ad, for example, is legendary. In becoming Internet memes, the surviving Soviet commercials curated by Retro Soviet Ads (among others) have finally found an informational ecosystem in which their value and appeal makes sense.

Once actual commerce took off in the former Soviet Union, commercials were not far behind. Television producers threw themselves into a desperate battle for their viewers, often outdoing their Western models in catering to a presumably shrinking attention span. From 1998 to 2000, the national TV channel RTR had a talk show called "Hakuna Matata," which livened up what was essentially an hour-long group conversation with constant, unmotivated changes in camera angles and frequent cuts to video of a young man roller-blading around the stage.

As for the commercials, while some of them were literally identical to their Western counterparts, as a phenomenon, they were assimilated differently. At first, commercials benefited from sheer novelty; in the early 1990s, when television channels still featured announcers reading to the camera from pieces of paper held in their hand, broadcasters would inform viewers that, say, "from 17:40 to 17:45 there will be a series of commercials." Initially, this meant the continual rerunning of a relatively small number of ads, whose slogan and catchphrases would not only be memorized by millions of viewers but become part of a mimetically expanding urban folklore of their own. Thanks to a nonsensical Snickers ad, anyone who heard the phrase "Ne tormozi" ("Don't hit the breaks!") would feel compelled to respond "Snikersni!" (The imperative of a made-up verb based on the word "Snickers.")

Commercials in the mid-1990s filled some of the memetic space left empty by the post-Soviet decline in political jokes. The 1994 ad campaign for the MMM pyramid scheme featured a set of easily identifiabe characters whose catchphrases entered daily conversation ("I'll buy the wife some shoes!" "Imagine that! They weren't tricking us!" "I'm not a freeloader, I'm a partner").[7] From 1992 to 1997, director Timur Bekmambetov made a series of sixteen historically themed commercials for a bank called "Imperial." Sumptuously shot, they were brief vignettes about key figures in world history, with no obvious connection to banking except the tagline "Imperial Bank" at the end. An ad depicting a banquet hosted by Catherine the Great begins with Catherine saying, "And why isn't Count Suvorov eating anything?" Suvorov responds that the religious fast day is not over until the first star appears in the sky. Catherine's line became a hugely popular meme, spawning numerous parodies and serving as a catchphrase even to this day.

The late 1990s also saw experiments with a television show whose format—a mixture of paid, amateurish advertisements and egregiously bad performances by ordinary people desperate to be on TV—was basically YouTube before YouTube: *Znak kachestva* ("The Seal of Quality"). *Znak kachestva* began on TV-6 in August 1996 as a twice-daily, ten-minute series of clips, was transformed into a more traditional, hour-long format in June 1999, and finally canceled in early 2001 for poor ratings. Though it contained echoes of decades-long Soviet traditions of amateur productions (*khudozhestvennaia samodeiatel'nost'*) and talent shows (KVN), *Znak kachestva* was a revolutionary experiment in the democratization of television, winning viewers throughout the country and acclaim as far away as Japan. The idea behind *Znak kachestva* is deceptively simple: to allow anyone and everyone the opportunity to sing, dance, or recite poetry on national television at no charge. In addition, for a small fee, *Znak kachestva* also included announcements and advertisements in the same format (individuals standing in front of the camera rather than prerecorded commercial clips). *Znak kachestva* played a complicated game with its audience, inviting them both to identify with and mock the people on screen, who were essentially audience members who might have been better off never leaving their couches.

Thanks to the evolution of Russian media in the 1990s, the culture was already primed for Internet memes. All it needed was the Internet.

For the first dozen years of the century, the Russian Internet (Runet) was mostly unsupervised, with censorship and news manipulation limited primarily to television (still the main source of news for the average citizen of the Russian Federation today). Thus it became an outlet for satire and cynicism, as well as just ordinary playfulness. The same DIY culture of video sharing, multimedia parodies, and meme creation familiar in the West could (and still can) be easily identified on the Runet.

CHAPTER 3
LOOKING BACKWARD
A MEME'S EYE VIEW OF RUSSIAN
HISTORY AND CULTURE

The American podcast "Reply All" featured a regular segment called "Yes Yes No," in which hosts Alex Goldman and P. J. Vogt unpacked a new nugget of Internet culture for their company's founder, Alex Blumberg. More often than not, the focus was on either tweets or memes. Blumberg was stumped by most if not all of the references made by a given Internet meme, while Goldman and Vogt could usually explain all of them (with occasional help from guests).

This weekly ritual enacted one of the things Internet memes do best: drawing the boundaries between the in-group who understands them and the rest of the world that does not. Depending on their referents, Internet memes can be enjoyed by a very small, niche audience or by the broader public. Thanks to their referentiality, Internet memes function like riddles: a riddle hides a familiar object behind an unfamiliar description, and the pleasure is in the realization of how the trick worked. To understand the riddle, you must already know the hidden object. You only "get" a riddle if you've already "gotten" it.

The audience-defining function of the Internet meme is one of the things that make another culture's memes worth examining. A given national, ethnic, or language group's Internet memes will depend on shared backgrounds and cultural codes. A great deal of cultural labor in Russia since 1991 has centered on reexaminations of the country's past, whether it be thorny questions of history (such as Stalin's purges) or the enduring value of Russian high culture in a capitalist entertainment economy. (We must always remember the great Russian writers!) These debates are usually framed by experts with institutional authority: scholars, journalists, politicians, and educators; the role of the public is to express opinions that horrify said experts, thereby keeping the debates going.

The Internet's liberating political power may have been overstated by post-Cold-War techno-utopians, who assumed that computer networks and social media would always be effective challenges against tyranny. But the Runet has certainly democratized access to the conversations about compelling historical and cultural issues. It is not expertise, rhetorical persuasiveness, or even a way with words that compel netizens to entertain a comment on the country's cultural heritage; rather, it is a matter of selecting images, usually combined with just a few words (often preexisting set phrases). Clever commentary no longer depends as much on language.

At the same time, however, there is as much continuity as there is rupture. Take, for example, the memes about Soviet leaders (Lenin, Stalin, Khrushchev, Brezhnev, and Gorbachev).[1] In the world of Russian humor, this is well-trodden ground, as anecdotes about each one of these men were among the most popular jokes in the postwar Soviet Union. When they become the subjects of Internet memes, they bring a number of familiar tropes from Soviet anecdotes along with them but also start to cover new ground.

Jokes about Lenin tended to play off the cult of the Soviet founder that developed under Stalin. After Lenin's death, his corpse was put on display in a mausoleum in Red Square, where it lies to this day. Lenin occupied a peculiar space in the Soviet symbolic system: state propaganda insisted on his "immortality" (i.e., his ideas and work live on), while the iconography was built literally over his dead body:

"Let's go to the theater! They're performing Tolstoy's play, *The Living Corpse!*"
"Enough already! Why does everything have to be about Lenin?"

Lenin comes back to life and goes to a bar to hang out with the proletariat. The works stand around drinking, and pay no attention to him.

Lenin: "So, comrades, you don't recognize me!"
One of the workers: "Vanya, take a look! It's the 10-ruble bill!"

While Lenin Internet memes cover a wide range of topics, they expand on the themes of death and immortality that were already present in Soviet jokes by taking advantage of the many familiar visual images of the Soviet leader as a corpse or a monument. In one, Lenin lies in his tomb with a cat on his belly, saying he's afraid to move as he'll wake the cat. In another, Lenin's corpse is accompanied by the phrase "Just five more minutes," as if his alarm had just gone off.

Another set of Lenin memes exploit a now famous photograph that was only released during Perestroika: Lenin in a wheelchair after his stroke, looking almost brain dead as he stares at the camera. The memes are captioned, "We're fucked comrades," "Let's pretend it didn't happen," "Vova, are you going to have anything else? Vova? Vova?"

Like many of the jokes, these memes put the lie to the crucial Soviet slogan, "Lenin lived! Lenin lives! Lenin will live!" This phrase was a fascinating exercise in magical thinking, considering how much of Soviet official culture revolved around the man's corpse. Back in the 1920s, the belief that communist science would conquer death may not have been entirely a fringe idea, but it certainly receded a decade later; the slogan remained.[2] One meme uses the repeated image of Lenin (twelve in all) to anchor a joke that emphasizes how empty these words are. On a chart with basic tenses on the vertical axis (Past/Present/Future) and more complex variations on the horizontal (Simple/Continuous/Perfect/Perfect continuous). The top row reads: "Lenin was alive. Lenin lived for some time. Lenin lived, but then stopped. Lenin lived for some time, and then died." Deprived of actual content, all that is left of the slogan is grammar.

In addition to Soviet jokes, some Lenin memes tapped into the vein of absurdist humor and performance art that started to reach the public consciousness during Perestroika. In May 1991, Sergei Kuryokhin, a multitalented musician, composer, and performance artist, and reporter Sergei Sholokhov broadcast a hoax interview on national television arguing that Lenin had consumed such large quantities of the fly agaric psychedelic mushroom that, by the end of his life,

Lenin was a mushroom himself. Panicked viewers call the studio for clarification.[3] Decades later, we have a meme with Lenin's head crowned by a mushroom cap and the words "Lenin was a mushroom, Lenin is a mushroom, Lenin will be a mushroom." Though perhaps the best memetic response is simply one of the standard pictures of Lenin, with the caption, "No, you're a mushroom!"

Stalin memes, while also consistent with earlier Soviet jokes, tend to be much more straightforward: the punch line is usually about executing people. Sometimes the sentence is mitigated to exile, with a number of memes about sending people to Siberia, and others making puns on the fact that the word for "exile" is the same as the word for "footnote." Occasionally, the memes play off of his bloodthirsty reputation more subtly, such as in the meme of Stalin smoking his pipe: "When Comrade Stalin smoked, the Ministry of Health didn't make a peep." Or they use Stalin as a reminder of how things have changed: "We didn't have any of this bullshit when I was around." And, of course, they get meta, as seen in another image of Stalin smoking his pipe: "Comrade Stalin approves of your interior monologue."

Though Lenin and Stalin also feature in English-language memes, their deployment is quite different. Lenin is the subject of a wide range of "Hey, girl" memes, while the standard images of Stalin as leader of the USSR are intermixed with a popular set of memes feature Stalin as a youth. This famous picture of a dashingly handsome Stalin wearing a scarf around his neck is commonly known as "Hipster Stalin." Sometimes he wears Warby Parker glasses, and usually, the joke is about liking or doing something "before it was cool."

The visual component of memes about Soviet leaders adds new layers of possible humor (since the joke doesn't have to be entirely verbal), but at the same time, the range of subject matter looks a bit narrower than in the Soviet anecdotes. In this regard, the memes are reminiscent of the politically themed matryoshka dolls that Russian vendors have been hawking to tourists since the last days of the USSR: each nesting doll represents one of the Soviet leaders, which means there is only one opportunity to make a joke or tell a story about each one. For example, Nikita Khrushchev would be painted either holding a shoe (the primary association in the minds of Westerners), an ear of corn (the primary association in the mind of ex-Soviets), or both. The Internet memes occasionally play with the famous shoe-banging incident from Khrushchev's speech at the United Nations, but since their audience is Russian speakers, most of the memes make reference to the post-Stalinist leader's legendary preoccupation with planting corn on land that had never grown it before. Some of the memes involve sexual humor (thanks to the corncob's phallic shape), but even without this particular form of low comedy, Khrushchev seems to have either a fetish for or love affair with corn.

But it is Brezhnev who is most transformed by the movement from anecdotes to meme. Of all the Soviet leaders, Brezhnev is the one whose appearance and physical presence provide at least as much material as his words. The anecdotes about Brezhnev usually focused on his slow, halting, and slurred speech (particularly prominent in his last decade, after he likely suffered a stroke). The Brezhnev of the Soviet joke could barely formulate a sentence and had only a vague notion of what was going on around him. One of the few easily translatable Brezhnev jokes has him tottering to the podium in order to open the 1980 Olympics in Moscow. Brezhnev stares straight ahead, intoning, "O! O! O!" Finally, an aid rushes to his side, telling him, "Leonid Ilich! That's not the teleprompter—that's the Olympic Symbol."

The Internet memes, by contrast, pay little attention to his manner of speaking, focusing instead on his appearance. This makes sense: the best part of a Brezhnev joke was hearing the teller's imitation of Brezhnev, while most of the memes have no sound. But they do have his droopy face and world-famous unibrow. His expressionless visage lends itself to easy comedy, as in one meme that turns him into the Terminator. But mostly, the Internet memes are visual and verbal jokes about the Soviet general secretary's propensity for kissing other (male) world leaders on the lips. Long found amusing in the West, Brezhnev's kisses were immortalized on the eastern side of the Berlin Wall in 1990 by the artist Dmitri Vrubel, who painted reproduction of a famous photograph of Brezhnev kissing East German leader Erich Honecker. Entitled "God Help Me to Survive This Fatal Attraction," Vrubel's graffiti, which decontextualized a well-known image, prefigured the aesthetics of the Internet meme; the main difference was that Vrubel's picture, rather than bouncing through the ether, was literally set in stone. The caption to one recent meme reads, "Long before [Harvey] Weinstein, Brezhnev made people kiss him in public." In another, Brezhnev is photoshopped into the iconic picture of an upside-down Spider-Man kissing Mary Jane Watson (Brezhnev is MJ), while yet another presents a gallery of the four "most beautiful kisses": Spider-Man and Mary Jane, Jack and Rose on the Titanic, Han Solo and Leia, and Brezhnev and Honecker. Even when Brezhnev isn't actually kissing, the memes suggest he's thinking about it: "Let me kiss you!"; "I'm a simple man. I see a mouth, I kiss it!"

The emphasis on the visual also has its effect on memes about classic Russian writers. The undisputed paragon of the Russian literary tradition is Alexander Pushkin (1799–1837), even though his work does not travel as well as that of Dostoevsky or Tolstoy, since most of it is in verse. In addition to short poems, his output included dramas, comedies, narrative poems, short stories, and *Eugene Onegin*, a novel in verse. To this day, reverence for Pushkin is cultivated (if not required) by the Russian school curriculum, and many Russian citizens of all generations can quote his poems by heart (the fact that so many have been set to music doesn't hurt).

Arguably, there is also something stultifying about the cult of Pushkin, whose seriousness makes it easy to forget just how playful much of the poet's work actually was. When the former dissident writer Andrei Sinyavsky (Abram Tertz) wrote a breezy, irreverent book called *Strolls with Pushkin*, it was met with outrage—even when it was published in the Russian Federation after the collapse of the USSR.[4] Sinyavsky was not the first to treat Pushkin with humor rather than undiluted adoration; in the 1920s and 1930s, the absurdist poet Daniil Kharms wrote several "Anecdotes about Pushkin," in which Pushkin displays a bizarre obsession with throwing rocks, or in which he has four sons ("all idiots"), and keeps falling off of chairs because he doesn't know how to sit in them right.[5] In 1990, Yuri Mamin directed a film called *Sideburns* (*Bakenbardy*) about young men who, determined to save Russia from vice, dress up in nineteenth-century garb and form a club of "Pushkinists." In a particularly famous moment, a sculptor who has spent his life making statues of Lenin demonstrates that he can change a Lenin head into a Pushkin head in just under thirty seconds.

Some of the Pushkin memes are about the duel that led to the poet's death, but what is most striking is how often the memes about Pushkin emphasize his race. That Pushkin's great-grandfather was African is a well-known fact; the early twentieth-century poet Anna Akhmatova refers to the young Pushkin as a "swarthy youth."[6] But his African heritage had no real impact on the understanding of Pushkin as essentially *Russian*, with great emphasis given to the role of his peasant nanny and the Russian folktales she told him as a boy.[7] In any case, in a country with a negligible population of African descent, the question of Pushkin's ancestry was far less racialized than an American would expect.

This is not the case for Russian meme-makers. Again and again, Pushkin is not just "African" or even Black—his image is transfigured into African American stereotypes, particular those associated with gangsta rap. In one, he is dressed as a hip-hop DJ, accompanied by the quote, "Everyone follows his own nature." In another, he flashes a gang sign and says "yo" under the caption "When you're just talking and discover that you're rhyming." In yet another, he is dressed in full hip-hop regalia; "This is you when you've found a new rhyme and go for it." The same image is used for a meme that lays bare the logic behind the Pushkin hip-hop memes: "The first Russian rapper wasn't Timati; the first Russian rapper was A.S. Pushkin. His rhymes were dope, he had African roots, and he died in a shoot-out." (Cf. a more unpleasant version, with a classic Pushkin portrait: "I died like a real n****r—in a shoot-out.")

The irreverent Internet culture has no problem undercutting the pieties of the Pushkin cult by reframing him as "ghetto." On the whole, meme-makers have little interest in patrolling the boundaries between high and low culture, nor are they concerned about racism. The implicit denigration of Black people while enjoying and appropriating Black culture is hardly unique to Russia.

The racism of these memes is not incidental. They perform some fascinating cultural work: we end up with a complex reconfiguration of Russian cultural patrimony on the global stage. The African roots of the greatest Russian writer have never undermined his Russianness, and the fact that he was both Black by American standards and a poet can legitimate a connection to the international dynamo of hip-hop. Russia has a growing number of its own hip-hop performers (including Timati, referenced in one of the memes), and none of them is Black. Given Russian demographics, that is hardly surprising, but Pushkin, the part-African genius of Russian literature, becomes a bridge between hip-hop and Russia.

The track-suited, rhyme-spitting Pushkin makes manifest a dynamic already visible in many of the memes about Soviet leaders: the collision of historical figures and present-day concerns in Russian Internet memes makes the past come alive. All of these subjects of historical memes end up inserted in a familiar meme macro, which juxtaposes the historical figure's image with some (usually negative) scene from today's world, and the tagline "How's [X] working out for you?" No one should expect historical accuracy from Internet memes, but this macro suggests that the meme-makers are not even trying: the anachronism is often the point. These absurd juxtapositions are implicit statements not just about history but about the present day.

CHAPTER 4
FOLK HEROES OF THE RUNET

The Milkman Cometh

In August 2014, as Russia was only beginning to adjust to the sanctions imposed by the United States and Europe after the seizure of Crimea, viewers throughout the Russian Federation found themselves charmed by an American farmer and small businessman. His name was Justus Walker, but he was quickly dubbed the Jolly Milkman (веселый молочник).

Walker, who ran a farm in the Krasnoyarsk region with his (American) wife, was being interviewed about the effect of the government's policy of "import substitution" on his business. In excellent Russian, he explained:

> When we would talk to customers in the city, they would say, "So why should I buy your mozzarella? I can buy Italian, and it's not much more expensive. Let's say, 900 rubles a kilo, instead of 650. So why should I?"

> And now, well, why should you? Because there won't be any of that Italian cheese of yours![1]

Whereupon he burst into inordinately loud laughter.

The public's embrace of Walker was a huge phenomenon that, despite its beginnings on state television, played itself out largely on the Internet. A cartoon rendering of his laughing face made its way into online meme generators, with Walker's image now available to comment on virtually any question. From "And you won't have any personal life . . . Ahahahaha!" to "Because there won't be any more of your 'Game of Thrones,'" Walker could be relied upon for a joyous, almost nihilistic response. But why?

Justus Walker was an unusual combination of the familiar and the exotic, de-fanging and domesticating a foreign threat behind a lovable, goofy facade. It would have been easy to make someone like Justus into the enemy, thanks to his unusual backstory. Homeschooled by his evangelical missionary parents in Iowa, he moved with them to Russia in 1994, when he was turning eleven. This, of course, is the perfect age for linguistic adaptation: he managed to master Russian as a second native language, presumably with no detriment to his first.[2] Six years later, when his parents went back to the United States, Justus stayed behind.

Perhaps the passage of time helped. The post-Soviet influx of missionaries, Protestant and otherwise, was greeted with hostility by many in the Russian Federation, particularly the leaders of the Russian Orthodox Church. A succession of increasingly restrictive laws on religion put a stop to most of this proselytism, while the persecution of Jehovah's Witnesses and followers of other faiths deemed to be "totalitarian sects" (cults) has picked up in recent years.[3] But it is no longer the hot-button issue that it used to be. Given the state and the media's agitation for "traditional values" and fear-mongering about LGBT people, salt-of-the-earth family men like Justus Walker (with his three children) start to look like role models.[4]

Justus Walker would never have gone viral without his boisterous, slightly off-putting laughter, but his memetic staying power suggests there might be more to it. At a time when the United States and the liberalism it represented were being increasingly demonized, here was an American who had chosen to become Russian, embodied traditional values, lived in the heartland, and was doing his part for the domestic economy dealing with a collapse of foreign trade. His nickname only furthers his Russification. Since 2000, the Russian Vimm-Bill-Dann company has sold a line of dairy products (milk, yogurt, sour cream, cream cheese) whose symbol is the cartoon drawing of a smiling, mustachioed fat man in an apron and a chef's hat, and whose slogan is "Tasty food, good mood." The brand is called "The Jolly Milkman," making the laughing Justus Walker's nickname virtually inevitable. The memes, which tended to feature him callously but infectiously laughing off one tragedy after another, are the marriage of stereotypical American optimism and equally stereotypical Russian fatalism.

Of course, he became the happy face of "import substitution." Thanks to the course his life has taken, he personally embodies it.[5]

Casting Call

The Jolly Milkman is only one of many beloved characters who populate the virtual land of Russian memes. This should be no surprise to anyone familiar with Internet memes throughout the world. Millions of people know the Most Interesting Man in the World, Pepe the Frog, the Distracted Boyfriend, Grumpy Cat, Nyan Cat, the Dramatic Chipmunk and Doge. For Americans, at least, the birth of these characters as Internet memes was also the rebirth of a particular type of folklore that had been largely dormant. Certainly, characters from popular entertainment had long had a crowdsourced afterlife in the world of fan fiction, but fan fiction was (1) a niche phenomenon for those in the know, and (2) not particularly conducive to short, pithy burst of texts or imagery to be broadly shared.

The Russian context, however, shows the missing link between Internet memes and earlier folk cultures: the joke. By the second half of the twentieth century, the traditional joke in America (set up followed by punch line) had fallen out of favor. Humor was observational and persona-based rather than portable; comedians did not tell jokes in the manner of their borscht-belt ancestors. Children still had their specific, transgressive joke genres (dead baby jokes, Helen Keller jokes), but jokes about stock character types (one of the ancestors of the character-based Internet meme) had fallen out of favor. They were not just old-fashioned, but, increasingly, they were recognized as offensive. Ethnic jokes had become taboo in the last few decades of the last century, while attempts at finding groups that were available for stigmatization (replacing "Polaks" with "dumb blondes," for instance) were less and less successful.[6]

Meanwhile, In Russia

None of this was the case with Russian joke culture. Not only were Russian speakers far more comfortable with ethnic humor and less likely to take offense, but they also, as the previous chapter indicated, took great pleasure in sharing portable, context-independent anecdotes that sometimes, but not always, centered on familiar stock characters. Where the heroes of English-language Internet memes seemed to come from nowhere, Russian memetic protagonists had a more immediate ancestry. Everyone knew Red Army Commander Chapaev and his comrades, Petya and Anya, Russian Civil War film heroes who lived on in endless anecdotes based on the commander's gnomic pronouncements, which fell somewhere between profundity and stupidity. Everyone knows Vovka the schoolboy scamp, Rabinovich the clever Jew, and Stirlitz the Soviet undercover agent in Nazi Germany. Like Internet memes, the jokes featuring these characters worked through a combination of revisitations of the familiar (the characters) and some strange new context. In the early 1990s, many Russians complained that the anecdote form seemed to have died along with the USSR, but by the decade's end, new stock characters such as the tacky rich New Russians joined their predecessors and helped revive the genre.

Though some of the heroes of anecdotes had their roots in film, they all functioned as primarily verbal artifacts: drawing pictures of Stirlitz or Rabinovich might be fun, but it was hardly necessary. Before the Soviet collapse made collecting the jokes in book form possible, their memetic survival depended on person-to-person transmission. Jokes made their way to the burgeoning new Internet, of course; one of the first Russian websites was anekdot.ru. But it was the Internet meme that effectively ported the community-affirming function of joke-telling to the new platforms of social media, freeing the joke-telling impulse from the limitations of an exclusively verbal existence. The Internet meme in Russia was the evolution of the anecdote into a multimedia format. Like the Jolly Milkman, the new Internet meme heroes came from unexpected sources: not just TV broadcasts but Flash animation, YouTube clips, repurposed photographs, to name just a few. They are the cultural touchstones of Russia's post-Soviet generations. This chapter will introduce you to the best and the worst of them.

A Quick Chat with the Local Lunatic

Scholars such as Limor Shifman and Bradley E. Wiggins have begun what is surely the open-ended process of defining the various genres of Internet memes.[7] Most of them cross national boundaries easily, with certain formats, screenshots, and cartoon images serving as immediately recognizable templates.

But formal characteristics are not the only means by which to categorize memes. One of the most successful kinds of video memes throughout the world simply provides a platform for people who might generously be called eccentric. This kind of generosity is sadly rare in MemeWorld, so there is no point in being overly delicate: the people in question often appear mentally ill, neurodivergent, or just profoundly strange. Residents of big cities (especially metropolitan areas with vast poverty and a poor mental health infrastructure, such as nearly every city in the United States or Russian Federation) may find the subjects of these videos familiar, in that these memes are a kind of "greatest hits" collection of the sort of interactions one might occasionally have on the street. The difference, of course, is the medium: the camera that records them and the network that distributes them keep their subjects at a safe distance while doing little to encourage empathy.

These memes are less likely to be uploaded cell phone videos; more often than not, they are television "man on the street" interview gone wrong. One of them, recording in 2010 in Minsk (Belarus), became such a phenomenon that it threatened to define the whole category: a conversation with a middle-aged woman wearing an extravagant, red conical headdress she referred to as a "Kandibober."

"Kandibober" is an unusual word in Russian; even those who are familiar with it are not all that likely to use it. It connotes something striking, unusual, and either fashionable or attempting to be fashionable; it is like the phrase "bells and whistles," but referring to personal style. And the woman who used the word in the video definitely had that.

One of the things that make the Kandibober video work is the disconnect between the words the woman says and her manner of saying them. She is poised and well-spoken, if slightly unusual looking, and seems prepared to launch into a lecture. The launch, however, fails spectacularly.

The reporter was simply stopping people on the street and asking them about the rare names they've encountered during their lives.

> WOMAN: (giving it some thought). How do I explain . . . (she smiles). I've lived a long life. . . . Does the name Ibrahim mean anything to you? A wonderful name. Allahu akbar.
> REPORTER: Thank you.
> WOMAN: I went through the Afghan War. And I wish all men [the chance] to go through it. A man is defined by his deeds, not his words. And if I wear a kandibober on my head, that doesn't mean I'm a woman or a ballerina.[8]

Her words are like a selection of superdense avant-garde poetry; it almost seems that, with the proper scholarly apparatus (footnotes, glossaries), all of this would make sense. "Ibrahim" is an answer to the initial query, but her own question ("Does the name Ibrahim mean anything to you?") suggests that it has some greater significance. Dropping in "Allahu akbar" muddies things further, but at least it connects to her next sentence about the Afghan War. Here, though, we are suddenly confronted with a confusing set of statements about gender: she went through the Afghan War. This is possible for a woman her age, if not statistically likely. In other words, her very presence there as a woman makes her something of an outlier. But she insists on defining the experience entirely in terms of masculinity, even as her phrasing makes it sound as though the Afghan War were still going on in the twenty-first century. The declaration about men's deeds and words is entirely conventional, if unexpected. Yet, it is a definition of manhood that is performative ("deeds") rather than purely essentialist. Thus her conclusion about what she wears on her head not meaning she's a woman or a ballerina is also tied to performance, while leading some commentators to wonder if this means that she is not "actually" a cisgender woman. (The terms used in the YouTube comments are much less temperate.)[9]

Thus, in addition to constantly verging on nonsense, the "Kandibober" monologue destabilizes viewers by never letting them be sure exactly what (whom) they are seeing. The entire performance verges on camp; the woman, like the word "Kandibober" itself, is a sign of extravagant, artificial excess. Sadly, any speculation that she is transgender only intensifies her framing as a freakish object of fascination in a cultural context that is primed to equate gender nonconformity with aberration or mental illness. Nor could her gender identity serve as a complete explanation for her words, which would be puzzling no matter who said them.

"Kandibober" became an Internet sensation. Agnia Ogonek, a YouTuber with a channel dedicated to memes,[10] notes that when the video first made it onto the Internet, it was primarily as fodder for YouTube Poops (video mashups), until late in 2010, when a YouTuber calling himself Max +100500[11] featured it in his overview of recent memes (his response to the Afghan War section: "Shit! Now I'll have to make a time machine to go back and go through the Afghan War"). Users all over the Russian Internet made their own version of the interview.

Image macro memes soon followed, mostly about either the Afghan War ("Be a Man, goddammit! Go through the Afghan War") or the gender confusion, most strikingly, an image of Putin wearing the famous headdress, with Medvedev telling him he looks "like a broad" and Putin responding, "If I wear a kandibober on my head, that doesn't mean I'm a woman or a ballerina." Users online speculated about her mental health, her name and occupation (with one theory placing her as a teacher in a high school), and whether or not she might have once served in the Afghan War as a man. A decade later, her fame lives on, particular in a VKontakte group called "The Church of the Great Kandibober,"[12] which has created an entire mock theology (although it has shown great ecumenism by branching out to other famous memes on its VK page). "Kandibober"-themed shopping bags and T-shirts are still available online.

The Kandibober lady was spotted and recorded several years later on a bus, but, sadly, the Kandibober was nowhere in sight. Much more distressing was the content of the video itself: with the passage of time, and in this very different context, she appeared disheveled and disturbed. The resulting recording, though available all over the Internet, is something I'm reluctant to call an Internet meme. Its memetic survival strategy depends on the original clip and has an appeal that is limited to simply satisfying the viewers' curiosity about where the Kandibober lady is now. The first video had the charm of short, unexpected conversation with an eccentric who, whatever else you might say about her, looks happy. In the second, any qualms the viewer might already have about laughing at her should now be hard to ignore.

The Kandibober video had other sequels, though they did not feature the first video's breakout star. Rather, "Kandibober" becomes not just a meme but a meta-meme: a genre of memes that we can identify thanks to the popularity of the original. Several clips were subsequently poJacksted on YouTube with names like "Kandibober 2," "Kandibober 3," and "Is this the New Kandibober?" The vagueness of the word "Kandibober" itself helps make this meme a productive category, in that "Kandibober" now implicitly refers to an unusual extravagance manifested verbally rather than visibly.

The "sequel" videos featured a rotating cast of characters, including a woman from Ulyanovsk whose answer to a question about Victory Day turned into a long disquisition ending with her casual announcement that in a few years she will be president of the Russian Federation.[13] Other "interview fails" that were not explicitly called "Kandibober" were memetically quite successful, including an aggressive, possibly drunken middle-aged woman on a bus, who claimed she was a marine and kept telling the driver to "start" driving (as if they were in a race) before cursing him out and telling him, "By the way, you're fired.[14] One of the more famous ones starts as an interview and ends as an interview photobomb: the old man referred to as "Uncle Bom Bom," thanks to his strange insistence that everything will be "Bom bom." Uncle Bom Bom calls the interview an "Indian" and then keeps interrupting the next interview of a young woman.[15]

If reporters were actually hunting for the next viral video stars, one could find worse strategies than interviewing random passers-by, especially during a live broadcast. The appeal resides in the unpredictable randomness of the individual in the crowd. It is fruitless to generalize about the Kandibober lady because her specificity is precisely the point. Moreover, the questions she and her colleagues in eccentricity were asked are thoroughly innocuous, so any detours they make into politics or world affairs only highlight the interview subject's oddness.

Not long after Kandibober, however, a new viral heroine made her debut on a stage that was explicitly political. Svetlana (Sveta) Kuritsyna, a nineteen-year-old woman from the provincial town of Ivanovo, was at the Metro station after just leaving a rally organized by the pro-Putin youth movement called "Nashi" in support of the country's ruling party, "United Russia." *Moskovskie novosti* correspondent Yevgeny Gladin asked a small group of participants if they would give him an interview, and he ended up recording Sveta on his iPhone. And so a new sensation was born: "Sveta from Ivanovo." In her own words:

> My name is Svetlana, from the city of Ivanovo. "United Russia" [Putin's party] had made very many accomplishments: they've raised put the econo ... economy, we've started to ... dress more better, and there wasn't what there is now—these are very big accomplishments! In agriculture everything's good. . . . There's more . . . land . . . more, well, . . . I don't know how to say it . . . more land sown . . . and, yeah, vegetables, rye—all of that. What else. . . . Since our country is multinational, we have lots of people in Moscow who help us a lot ... from other cities. . . . Yes, it's a big accomplishment! Very good, even! See, well. . . . See, back in Ivanovo medicine has gotten good . . . uh, what else . . . the cities are well-maintained . . . housing . . . no problems with that. People are helping very well.[16]

Within two weeks, the video had 2.5 million views on YouTube, ensuring Sveta fifteen minutes of fame that she did her best to stretch out for nearly two years.[17] After several television appearances, Sveta got her own reality show called *A Ray of Light* (in Russian, *Luch Sveta*, a play on her own name), which ran from June 2012 to June 2013. What was the secret of Sveta's unexpected success?

In part, it was the humor in watching a tongue-tied young woman do her best to express an orthodox political point of view without the requisite linguistic or intellectual skills. When tasked with enumerating United Russia's accomplishments, she vamps terribly. All she can do is run down a mental list of socioeconomic categories that have almost nothing to do with reality. "Our multinational country" is a cliché she probably remembered from school, and since she knows that agriculture must be important, she rattles off every crop she can think of. ("We've planted more rye" is a slogan even the Soviets would have rejected.) That her assertion about housing ("no problems with that") is counterfactual would be obvious to anyone who has spent any time in a Russian city. She is even less successful when choosing verbs and adjectives. ("It's a big accomplishment! Very good, even!" "People are helping very well!")

Sveta briefly became the face of Putinism at its most inarticulate. Her inability to elaborate a political platform was perfectly consistent with the ruling party's ideology before Putin's return to power in 2012: there was no clear program other than the continual expression of Russian "power" and "sovereignty." Just a few years later, that would change; Putin and United Russia recast themselves as the defenders of a traditionalist Russia against the godless, liberal forces that would undermine Russian statehood by weakening the family and encouraging the "gay agenda." Sveta and her blank stare would have been completely inadequate as the symbol of the country's new conservative turn.

Her viral fame was thus ensured by her insufficient mastery of two languages: the language of Putinism, native to none and impossible to master because of its internal contradictions, and ordinary spoken Russian. The feature common to most of the memes created in the wake of Sveta's Sermon at the Metro was her phrase "more better" (*bolee luchshe*), which flagrantly violates the grammatical norms of Russian (nor is it a common mistake). Photo after photo of women in hideous clothing got the caption "We've started to dress more better." One popular image macro of Putin and Medvedev laughing has them saying, "We've started to live more better!" Then adding, "But *you* haven't!" Another shows Sveta vacantly staring ahead, over the caption, "Under Putin, the dollar has started yielding more and more rubles" (i.e., the ruble is weaker). The same image rises in a ghostly form above a green field, with the caption, "yeah, vegetables, rye—all of that."

Sveta, the Kandibober lady, and their many companions in Internet fame are (presumably) real people whose memification turned them into recognizable characters. This process also works in the other direction, as the Internet is filled with fictional characters who became recognizable, productive memes.

This Little Piggy Gets the Fuck out of Rashka

Thanks to its origins, its style, and the unexpected cultural and political context it quickly acquired, a Russian Internet meme about an imaginative, wandering piglet became an instantly recognizable shorthand for giving up on Russia and finding a new country to call home. Preferably while using the foulest possible language to tell the tale.

Our story begins with a series of three children's books by one of Russia's most acclaimed living writers, Ludmila Petrushevaksya. Though her prose fiction and drama for adults are often gruesome and depressing (even as they are mixed with great humor and wit), her three children's books (*Peter Piglet and the Car, Peter Piglet and the Store,* and *Peter Piglet Pays a Visit,* all published in 2002) are innocuous enough. Like many a picture book hero, Peter is blessed with a powerful imagination that allows him to make the best of any situation; also typical is his love for all means of transportation. If Peter needs a tractor, he imagines one into existence—ditto for planes and cars.

In 2004, the books were scanned and uploaded to LiveJournal, where they soon spawned a series of parodies (including *Peter Piglet Goes to Hell* and *Peter Piglet in Silent Hill*). One particular image from the original book spawned a series of memes on dvach (2chan): Peter on his red tractor. Or, rather, as it came to be called, his "shitty tractor."

Six years later, a song about Peter Piglet made the essence of these memes clear while bringing the phenomenon to a much wider audience. The song wouldn't work without the memes, but the memes might not have spread as far without the song:

Stealing the fuck out of a shitty tractor,
I get the fuck out of Rashka (Russia)
Peter Piglet
In my white shirt

I'm fucking leaving
I'm fucking outta here
Stealing a fucking shitty tractor,
I see a miracle

Outside of Russia
I'll have lots of chicks
Here I'm a swine
But there I'm a Piglet

They'll love me
For my shirt
And for the tractor
That I stole out of fucking Rashka

Stealing a fucking shitty tractor,
I get the fuck out of Rashka (Russia)
Peter Piglet
In my white shirt[18]

Perhaps Peter was chosen because of the single-minded joy he seems to get out of simply driving in his (shitty) tractor. In Petrushevskaya's book, people come up to him and ask him questions, and he simply responds, "Sorry, I'm on a tractor" (as if that explains anything). It's worth noting that, even though Peter flies an airplane on the cover of one of the books, the Internet insists on keeping him in his tractor for a series of jokes about emigration. Wouldn't a plane be more sensible?

But that is also the point. Peter's imagination triumphs over base reality, and, oh, how base that reality is. His image has become firmly associated with the catchphrase, "Pora valit" ("Time to get out"), suggesting that things in Russia are going to hell. But Peter's blank-eyed optimism about his destination may be just as unwarranted as his belief that his "shitty" tractor can get him all that far. Peter Piglet may be driving in only one direction, but the meme's irony is more than capable of round trips.

On the one hand, there is the constant reference to "Rashka." A derogatory term for "Russia" combining the country's English-language name with a Russian suffix that can connote condescension or disdain, "Rashka" in recent years has become a fighting word. Patriots not only take offense at the term but tend to use it themselves as a way to denigrate liberals by attributing it to them. ("These are the sort of people who call our motherland 'Rashka.'") Like the Peter Piglet meme's irony, "Rashka"'s deployment is multidirectional. One meme makes this literal: Peter is riding his tractor out of Russia, while Gerard Depardieu, the French actor and Putin admirer who took Russian citizenship to avoid taxes, rides in. Each of them looks at the other and thinks, "He's fucking crazy!" (ebnutyi).

Yet Peter's presumed disdain for the motherland turns out to have an excellent pedigree, as demonstrated by a meme that has the piglet reciting a poem by nineteenth-century author Mikhail Lermontov: "Farewell, unwashed Russia, / Land of slaves, land of masters."

As the meme develops, any place that Peter leaves is "shitty" by definition. A chaos theory meme has Peter "getting the fuck out of this shitty world" by "stealing the fuck out of a strange attractor." In another, the forces of public order refuse to accept the "shittiness" of their home country. Peter is being chased by an indignant cop: "8000 a month is a normal salary! Turn around and come back!" In yet another, Peter is "getting the fuck out of King's Landing with Sansa Stark" (from *Game of Thrones*).

There is, however, something fundamentally tragic about the Peter Piglet series, in that Peter's happiness can never stand the test of time.

Meanwhile, In Russia

The initial message is about the shittiness of Rashka, but the cumulative effect of these memes is the realization that Peter Piglet is incapable of happiness, either because shittiness follows him wherever he goes, or because shittiness is the natural habitat he cannot do without. He is, after all, a pig, and many native speakers of English know that there is no one happier than a pig in shit.

Nothing works out for Peter when he leaves. A four-panel meme starts with Peter riding in his tractor, getting the fuck out of Rashka. The second panel has him proudly sending his friends pictures of himself from the first panel. But in the third: "And then—BAM!" His tractor crashes into something, which in the final panel turns out to be a giant tongue: "The language barrier."

Upon arrival, things are rarely better. True, in one meme, Peter is now in Germany, happily driving his shitty tractor around the Autobahn. But in another, Peter now has brown skin and is getting the fuck out of shitty Africa. In still another, Peter is welcomed into France, where he sits at a computer in a room he has decorated with a red star, a Soviet flag, and a portrait of Stalin. But Peter is not always trapped by nostalgia. One meme has him "getting the fuck out of America and going back to Russia," now that he has "stolen a better fucking tractor! It's patently obvious: Peter is a RUSSIAN" ("Rossianin"—the nonethnic word for a Russian citizen).

SpongeBob CrazyPants

Though any given Peter Piglet meme has a particular point of view about his home country, when taken together, these memes are ambivalent. You can take Peter Piglet out of "Rashka," but you can't take "Rashka" out of Peter Piglet.

This is not the case with another, even more famous "Rashka" themed meme that would arrive on the scene in 2011: Anton Chadsky's cartoon creation, Vatnik.

Nothing could be more ordinary than the phenomenon that the word "vatnik" normally described: a puffy, padded jacket filled with cotton. This jacket was a mainstay of the Soviet wardrobe (I hesitate to use the word "fashion" here), worn by Soviet soldiers during the winter months (from the 1940s through the 1960s), as well as forming part of the standard prisoner's uniform in the Soviet prison camp system (the Gulag). Chadsky made no bones about the political impetus behind the creation of the vatnik as cartoon drawings and Internet meme:

> It was in 2011, a couple of months before the mass protests against the falsified Duma elections. I decided to draw a character who would embody all the negative qualities of the typical Russian citizen (*rossianina*). By analogy to SpongeBob Square Pants, Rashka Square Vatnik (Рашка-Квадратный Ватник) was born.[19]

If "Rashka Square Vatnik" does not sound all that catchy in English, neither does "SpongeBob SquarePants" ("Gubka Bob Kvadratnye Shtany") in Russian. This meme is all about image. Chadsky drew Vanik to look like SpongeBob's angry, gray, drunken cousin. One of his eyes is always blackened, the other purple and closed shut. His snaggle-tooth rictus of rage is framed by a slovenly five-o-clock shadow.

Why is Vatnik so angry? A font of resentment, Vatnik is the mouthpiece for the reflexive, patriotic chauvinism one might expect from a soccer hooligan. But Chadsky's target is more general: the Putin-loving political majority whose members supposedly believe everything they hear on state television. Often depicted against the backdrop of the Russian tricolor flag, he parrots back propaganda in a joyful, drunken fury. He will tolerate no criticism of his country or of the Soviet Union. In one meme, we see him holding an icon of the Soviet Union's bloodiest leader, as he shouts, "If it weren't for Stalin, we would have all perished!" This particular strain of backward-looking patriotism is a common feature in the vatnik memes, in part because of timing: when the seventieth anniversary of the Soviet victory of the Nazis approached, the vatnik was already a familiar figure. Thus in one meme, vatnik leaps into the air, his arms joyously outstretched, shouting: "Hurrah! For our grandfathers! For Rus'! For Stalin! For Russian Orthodoxy! Victory!" In another meme featuring the identical pose, he says, "I broke the window in a German beer hall—got revenge for Grandpa! Hurrah for us!"

If Peter Piglet grows nostalgic for the chaos of his homeland, Vatnik lives in total squalor that he claims is paradise on earth. A common theme is to depict the vatnik in a decaying Russian village or filthy back alley as he spins conspiracy theories about the West's designs on his country: "The West wants to destroy Rosiushka" (nonsensical diminutive of "Russia"). This is consistent with Chadsky's own explanation of the catnip's ethos:

> Without hatred there can be no real vatnik. . . . Every vatnik tries to cover his hatred with noble motives or a wounded sense of justice, but we know.
>
> Here's what practically any vatnik hates:
>
> America in particular;
>
> The West as a whole;
>
> Sexual minorities . . .
>
> European values . . .
>
> Liberalism (because liberalism leads to European values; because liberals destroyed the USSR);
>
> Political and civil liberties (because these liberties— occupation by the West, a loss of OUR RESOURCES and the mandatory institution of debauchery starting in kindergarten);
>
> Dissent . . .
>
> Ukraine, Georgia, the Baltics, and all those AMERICAN WHORES, those countries that BETRAYED their Russian brother by choosing the civilized path of development. HOW DARE THEY?![20]

But even if we accept that the hatred is initially the product of Vatnik and the people he parodies, hatred inevitably becomes a two-way street. Loving Vatnik-as-parody is difficult to disentangle from hating the vatnik-as-object-of-parody. This raises the question: Is Vatnik an instrument of Russian self-hatred? The image of Vatnik is so hostile (however hilarious) that accusations of Russophobia begin to look rather credible.

On the surface (and in keeping with its creator's intent), the vatnik embodies the chauvinism and reflexive patriotism of Putin's Third and Fourth terms. As such, though, he is symptom as well as symbol: regardless of one's ideological mindset, the very fact of the vatnik points to the intense political polarization of Russia in the 2010s. Like the MAGA hat in the United States, his presence announces that the ideological battle lines have been drawn. There have been attempts at reappropriating vanity as a positive image for Putinists, with poems, songs, and videos of people declaring themselves to be Vatniki. But to the extent that this endeavor is successful, it occurs outside the world of Internet memes. The Vatnik meme is too laden with negative baggage to be rescued from liberal mockery.

What Does the Stoned Fox Say?

Vatnik and Peter Piglet may be vehicles for particularly jaundiced views of the culture that produced them, but there can be no doubt that these memes are Russian. Created by Russian speakers, they circulate primarily within the Russian Federation and the Russophone diaspora. Not all our examples, however, have such a straightforward genealogy.

What makes a Russian meme "Russian?" Surely, it has to be more than the presence of the Russian language; plenty of English-language memes get translated into other languages, Russian included, and many memes have no words whatsoever. Must they have identifiably Russian themes or tropes? That seems an undue burden; an American meme is American whether or not it has a flag, firearms, or football. Even the presence of famous Russians doesn't make a meme Russian: English-language memes featuring Putin (a topic for its own book) are not automatically Russian just because the country's president is featured (or lampooned).[21]

The hacker motto "information wants to be free" may seem like a relic of a more innocent time, but Internet memes certainly do their best to ignore the proprietary claims or borders of a given country. Take, for example, the transmedia metamorphoses of the hit television series *The Walking Dead*, which became serious meme fodder thanks to an image of the hero, Rick, and his teenage son, Carl. The original image's context is tragic: Carl has just left behind the corpse of his mother, on whom he had to perform a primitive, anesthesia-free C-section to save his unborn sister, only to put a bullet through his mother's head to prevent her from reanimating as a zombie. When Rick realizes what happens, he falls apart, gesticulating as he stands near Carl and cries. But the image looks as though he were berating Carl, giving rise to a popular image macro in which Rick says something topical or inane to Carl, and then repeats the main point while saying his son's name: "Snowballs, Carl!"

The show was popular in Russia, and so was the Russian version of the meme. These were not translations; some of the best "Carl" memes are puns, while others refer to something or someone in the public eye, so the Russian memes were distinctly Russian, even if their pattern came from the Anglophone online world. Even translated, many of these memes would mean nothing to a non-Russian audience (or, indeed, to an audience that hadn't been paying attention to the latest news). When photos from the February 2015 pre-Lent Maslenitsa holiday in Stavropol made their way onto the Internet the following month, users were amused and appalled to see an enormous version of the traditional holiday pancake (blin) baked in a pit. The blin, which was three meters in diameter, was scooped up and fed to celebrants with snow shovels. This became the source of one of the most popular Carl memes to hit the Russian Internet.[22] The next month, the popular opposition figure Alexei Navalny, as much an Internet figure as a politician, celebrated a successful campaign to have the new "Democratic Coalition" hold primaries, an unprecedented step in Russian politics. A picture of a smiling Navalny, standing in front of a sign saying, "Primaries, Karl!," amused many of his Twitter followers while puzzling others ("Who is Karl?").[23]

Thus one can look at the flow of Internet memes (and the material that inspires them) as a phenomenon of local adaptation and appropriation (the "Carl" meme), a complex multilateral trade (the "squatting Slav" meme in Chapter 6), or the exploitation of an aspect of a foreign "found object" that was not visible in its home environment. The best example of the latter case is the phenomenon known in Russian as "uporotyi lis," usually translated as "the Stoned Fox."

Like *The Walking Dead* and the Carl meme, the Stoned Fox was not originally Russian, nor was it initially a digital media phenomenon. The memification of the Stoned Fox reminds us that Internet memes, in addition to their lack of respect for national boundaries, circulate within the larger memetic context of human culture, in this case extending as far as physical objects. In 2012, a young Welsh artist and taxidermist named Adele Morse received a package containing the body of a fox that had got caught in a bear trap. Morse, a vegetarian with firm convictions about cruelty to animals, only worked with carcasses that were not killed for the purpose of taxidermy, which meant that her choice of subjects always had an element of the random built into them. She did not have any fox eyes, so she used eyes from a human doll, which may explain the uncanniness of the fox's appearance. Two years later, she put the fox on eBay, eventually selling it to Mike Boorman, a London DJ who displayed it during his gigs.[24]

Meanwhile, the fox had embarked on a digital life about which his creator was entirely unaware. The image she had posted to eBay found its way to the Runet, where it became one of the most popular subjects for photoshopping into other images in order to create memes. In Russian, this practice is called a "fotozhaba," based on a mispronunciation of "Photoshop" that sounds like it means "PhotoToad." Soon Morse started receiving emails with the memes, in which the fox joined Keanu Reeves, Joseph Stalin, Sigmund Freud, and Barack Obama. Eventually, the fox would hang out with Vladimir Putin, share lunch with construction workers on skyscraper beams, superimpose himself across a whole range of classic paintings (the Mona Lisa, riding Petrov-Vodkin's red horse), and insert himself into the Firefox logo. For an animal that never moved from his sitting position, the Stoned Fox certainly got around.

Russia has seen many Photoshop memes, before this one and certainly after. But the Stoned Fox was quickly mired in controversy, a surprise considering how innocuous the phenomenon was. At least one reason was an interview with Morse, in which she insists she was misquoted. In an interview published on March 13, 2013, on WalesOnline (not usually a top news source for residents of the Russian Federation), Morse spoke about the possible reasons for the fox's popularity:

"I asked what it was about the fox that they liked and he told me that the fox looks a bit sad and drunk and that's how Russians feel."

"His plastic eyes give him a glazed look and they identify with it, they think it symbolizes the nation."[25]

Whatever one might think of this particular interpretation, it was not Morse's own. But in the Russian press, this point of view was attributed directly to Morse herself. Morse quickly issued a denial. As she says in a 2014 interview on CrappyTaxidermy.com, "I got misquoted as saying it was because I thought all Russians were 'sad and drunk' this obviously A) is not something I would ever say and B) caused a massive reaction from Russians–rightly so."[26]

But the damage was done. In anticipation of an upcoming exhibit in Moscow and St. Petersburg, Morse was attacked by nationalists and conservatives of all stripes. Duma Deputy Vitaly Milonov, famous for his agitation against so-called gay propaganda, called the exhibit "propaganda for animal abuse," a charge the vegetarian Morse hotly denied (though she did express some pride at being targeted by such an odious figure). Milonov insisted that animals were only the beginning: "The next step is: they'll start stuffing humans and displaying them as art objects."[27] The leader of the St. Petersburg "Communists of Russia" affiliate accused Morse of "mocking our country" and "jeering at our national interests" by displaying the fox next to Lenin and other Russian leaders. A party spokeswoman called Morse an anti-Soviet(!) Russophobe.[28]

Fulminating against a stuffed fox and absurdist memes is a losing strategy; the accusers inevitably look laughable and humorless. Someone opened up a Russian-language Twitter account for the Stoned Fox: "Can someone tell me where Vitalik Milonov lives? We need to talk." "What's so anti-Russian about me? I don't get it. Are

your Russian Orthodox activists stoned?" ("Uporotyi lis pobyval").
The fox and Mike Boorman (the man who bought him on eBay) were
interviewed on the independent television station TV-Rain; Boorman
said that if the fox were given Russian citizenship, he would try to
legalize drugs so as to stay stoned. Host Pavel Lobkov, comparing the
fox to French actor Gerard Depardieu and American actor Steven
Seagal, responded that this meant the fox would never get citizenship
or a "five-room apartment in Grozny or Saransk."[29]

Intellectuals offered their own tentative theories about the fox's
popularity: the fox is a "meme you can touch" (Vladislav Tsyplukhin),
a freak show (Andrei Riabykh), an example of a Pavlovian response or
a chance to laugh at Putin (Ianina Ledovaia), a challenge to traditional
hierarchies (Boris Sokolov and Grigorii Tul'chinksi), or a senseless
image people insist on finding meaningful (Aleksandr Konfisakhor,
comparing the fox to Malevich's Black Square).[30]

Perhaps the most revealing response was that of the writer Georgii
Pankratov, who, in the business newspaper *Vzgliad,* insists that
"stupid" Internet memes are not worthy of exhibits. The fact that
Morse was invited is a sign that "something is rotten in society, where
such *fun,* such *have a nice time*" [italicized words are in English in the
original]. Comparing the Stoned Fox to the scandalous performance
by the feminist anarchist punk group Pussy Riot in the Cathedral of
Christ the Savior, Pankratov admits that the Stoned Fox is a minor
phenomenon, but that it is the sort of art that demands "repression":
"Formally, it is not breaking any laws besides 'morality,' [...] but in fact
it proves such a wave of disgust that one really wants to pass a law to
make sure that, if it happens now, it will never happen again."[31]

The reference to Pussy Riot is not accidental nor is the half-
hearted call for legislation. If the uproar over the Stoned Fox looks
disproportionate now, it is because late 2012 was a turning point in
contemporary Russian cultural politics. A wave of protests preceded
Putin's election to a third term, while the legislature was busily passing
law after restrictive law, eventually banning international adoption,
policing the Internet, forbidding swearing, and clamping down on so-
called homosexual propaganda. Inviting the creator of the Stoned Fox
to the country's capitals was like waving a red flag in front of a bull.

Representatives of the media and the state were primed to find sinister intent behind even the most vaguely subversive actions.

The years since 2012 have also been enough time for more and more of the country's population to grow comfortable with Internet culture. It is not that memes were unfamiliar; the "Witness from Friazino" meme (also a "fotozhaba," inserting a grim-looking young man in a wide range of photos) had been around since 2006 without causing an uproar. Still, the mere fact of sharing and enjoying memes in 2006 or even 2012 marked a user as Internet savvy and probably highly comfortable with irony. An identifiably "foreign" meme such as the Stoned Fox could still be seen as sinister by people who spent less of their lives online and who were already prone to see threats to their way of life around every corner. In terms of anxiety about memes, 2012–13 was something as an outlier. Memes are easier to domesticate than foxes (dead or alive); just one decade later, they are a recognized part of the Russian cultural landscape.

Wait, Wait . . . Don't Tell Me!

Just five years after the Stoned Fox, another bizarre European art object became a memetic hit in Russia, but this time it did not provoke outrage or controversy, despite the occasional interpretation of the meme's success as a reflection of the "Russian mentality." Instead, the meme was embraced wholeheartedly, praised as a national hero and quickly turned into the holy grail of capitalist culture: merch. This meme, which started on the Russian Reddit clone Pikabu in January 2017, is commonly called "Zhdun."

Though its appearance is bizarre, Zhdun is maximally non-threatening; gray and pear-shaped, Zhdun is always shown in a sitting position, its hands folded in its lap in a posture of patient waiting. Imagine a Teletubby dyed gray and with its head shrunken down to a quarter of its size, quietly passing the time and possibly nodding off at the Department of Motor Vehicles, and you have Zhdun.

As a post-Soviet phenomenon, Zhdun's origins were nearly as unlikely as those of the Stoned Fox. It began as a sculpture by the

Dutch artist Margriet van Breevoort, who installed a work entitled "Homunculus loxodontus" at the Leiden University Medical Center in 2016. In an interview, she explained its origins to a Russian reporter:

> I wanted to give it a scientific name, like a new species. Homunculus means "little guy" in Latin, or "artificially created human." And Loxodontus is the scientific name for African elephant, referring to the snout. I was commissioned by "Beelden in Leiden" to make something inspired by the LUMC, the medical center in Leiden, and I didn't want to create something about medicine or illness, but rather about the patients themselves. The way they just have to await their fate in the waiting rooms. About hoping for the best. [. . .] I wanted it to be a kind of lovable companion, something or someone that gives comfort, but also makes you laugh. In this building, there is also a lot of medical and genetic research going on. So the way the sculpture looks is a bit of a joke towards this research. It's like a failed experiment or product of this research that is hoping and waiting to get better. Like a big, cute, partly human and huggable lump of flesh.[32]

The story would have ended there, with a charming statue in front of a Dutch medical facility visited by a limited number of people, had a photo of van Brevoort's homunculus not somehow made its way onto Pikabu. While it is most famous under the Russian nickname "Zhdun," it acquired just as much popularity in Belarus and Ukraine. Known in Belarus as "Pochakun" and in Ukraine as "Pochekun," the Zhdun meme is an example of particularity (underscoring something specific to the local environment) without isolationism, and the meme's success in all three Slavic post-Soviet nations is a reminder of a shared cultural core that is free from any kind of Russian (post-) imperial hegemony..

Like the Stone Fox, Zhdun thrived in what became its new natural habitat: the fotozhaba. Indeed, one such meme has Zhdun sitting on a bench holding the Stoned Fox, while a confused John Travolta looks to his left and right, trying to figure out where he is. Zhdun has replaced FDR in the famous Yalta photo, where he sits between Churchill and Stalin. Indeed, anyone familiar with Russian memes by this point could predict where his image might next appear. Zhdun's face replaces that of the chubby-cheeked little girl on the classic Soviet chocolate bar Alyonka (itself a popular subject for fotozhaby). In keeping with the popular Russian memetic pattern of fotozhaby using famous paintings, Zhdun replaces the subjects of Valentin Serov's Girl with Peaches, Boris Kustodiev's Merchant Woman, Magritte's man with a green apple in front of his face, and, inevitably, the Mona Lisa (see Figure 1).

But Zhdun's appeal was not listed to the historical or the aesthetically distant. His posture of patient expectation lent itself to politics. In February 2017, a member of the Ukrainian Verkhovna Rada (the parliament) brought a stuffed "Pochekun" figure with him to the parliamentary meeting hall and parked him in front of a microphone.[33] Fotozhaby substituted Zhdun for Putin at cabinet meetings, for former Ukrainian prime minister Yuilya Timoshenko (complete with her signature braided-updo) waiting outside the bathrooms for Donald Trump to arrive, and for Trump himself behind the resolute desk, wearing the president's comb-over as he is surrounded by smiling well-wishers. A statue of Zhdun was even erected in front of the opulent residence of Ukrainian president Viktor Yanukovich, ousted during the Maidan protests of 2014.[34]

Figure 1 Zhdun reimagined as the Mona Lisa.

With no one defending the Zhdun trademark, the homunculus was featured in advertisements for real estate and credit cards and also ironically proposed as the mascot for the Russian postal service.

Why did Zhdun go viral? Why is his image photoshopped into an ever-widening array of classic paintings, photos, and random situations? The common denominator in every explanation I have seen is the phenomenon of waiting. From stereotypes about the Russian people's legendary patience to the Soviet experience of standing in endless lines, waiting appears to be a point of true commonality. Zhdun is claimed by Russia, Ukraine, and Belarus, despite the obvious political issues that can divide them. Zhdun seems to require no particular political affiliation. (The interview I quoted above was from Sputnik, a notorious Russian propaganda outlet.)

But it is also possible to see Zhdun as very much a creature of the present moment. Dmitry Travin writes:

> The conservative Zhdun thinks that the country's president had long been duped by government liberals, but now he has finally shaken them off and will accept an economic development program in the national interest. The liberal Zhdun thinks that the president had long been coopted by the siloviki, and didn't understand how bad things had gotten in our economy.

> [. . .]

> The young Zhdun is waiting for a change of elites and hopes to get a place in Gazprom. [. . .] The old Zhdun is waiting for order to be restored, for the enemies to be destroyed, for the USSR to be revived.[35]

All of this may be true, but in the context of the various post-Soviet identities examined so far, Zhdun is both an identity and a meta-identity. He is a rare national image with which everyone can identify, but that is because he also represents the very problem that stands in the way of a stable post-Soviet identity. He embodies the patient expectation of *something else*. Zhdun is placeholder for an identity, well aware that his function as a placeholder is in itself representative of a state of suspension that has been, for better or for worse, rather stable.

In this, he only makes sense as the herald of whatever comes next. His patience suggests a refreshing optimism about whatever that may be. After all, Zhdun would make a terrible forerunner of the apocalypse. No rough beast, slouching toward Bethlehem, he is a placid, cozy couch potato, content to sit wherever he has been left, staring straight ahead until something new starts to unfold before his wide-open eyes.

CHAPTER 5
MEMESTYLES OF THE RICH AND FAMOUS

Know Your Meme

Medieval kings are said to have had two bodies: the real, physical body, subject to all the cruel misfortunes that befall mere mortals (injury, aging, death), and the "body politic," the symbolic self with no biological history the public body of the business of state. When a human being becomes an Internet meme, they also exist in two separate realms that may intersect, but never entirely overlap. For people like Sveta from Ivanovo or the Kandibober lady, memification catapults them from anonymity to fame; in Sveta's case, her daily existence changed radically, but the Kandibober lady's did not. This is, in general, how celebrity works: the celebrity has a public body that belongs to everyone and carves out a separate life for their physical, everyday existence to varying degrees of success.

The phenomenon is different for people who are already famous. They were already public property before they became memes. The difference is that Internet memes constitute an entire sphere of public existence over which they can have virtually no control. Even the most skilled practitioners of public relations cannot "spin" an Internet meme; quite to the contrary, the more the subject of any online attention objects to the nature of the scrutiny or the content of the depiction, the more they help spread the very thing they would like to suppress.[1] Internet memes about famous people have the thrill of the carnivalesque: kings, queens, and movie stars are helpless before the mockery of common folk with a keyboard.

We have seen some examples of this sort of irreverence in the memes about Soviet leaders and Russian cultural luminaries, but in almost all those cases, the subjects of the memes had already lost control over the deployment of their own image when they left the land of the living. Their admirers may be offended on their behalf, but at a remove from the actual object of ridicule. It is a truism that dead men tell no tales; they also file no lawsuits.

It is now possible for a Russian citizen to be prosecuted for a satirical meme targeting a state official, thanks to a 2019 law banning "blatant disrespect" of the state, state officials, and state symbols, punishable by a 300,000 ruble fine and, for repeat offenders, fifteen days in jail. That October, a man was fined for posting a picture of graffiti someone else had written on the Yaroslavl police headquarters (the graffiti: "Putin is a f*ggot").[2] So far, this law, like so many of the repressive measures passed since 2012, has been enforced infrequently. Presumably, the strategy is not to go after every offender but to make people think twice before risking exposure to penalties.

Putin is an obvious target for criticism and satire and provides endless fodder for memes. In this chapter, we will examine a particular anti-Putin viral phenomenon that would certainly have run afoul of this legislation if it had already been on the books. But it would be a mistake to assume that satirical political memes are all aimed at the country's leadership. In contrast, we will also look at a similar memetic campaign against Barak Obama. In addition, we will see the political and ideological ramifications of viral content whose famous targets are not world leaders: the Swedish teenage climate activist Greta Thunberg and the American entrepreneur Elon Musk.

"Putin Is a Dickhead"

After twenty years in power, Putin is a gift to meme-makers. Internet memes depend on common points of reference; in Russia, what could be more universal than Putin? The "Putin is a Dickhead" meme is particularly attractive for analysis because it is a prime example of a meme that moves back and forth from "real life" to the Internet, with the added benefit of crossing national boundaries between Russian and Ukraine.

The Russian phrase "Putin—khuilo" is slightly challenging to render into English. "Khuilo" is not one of the most frequently used weapons in the vast linguistic arsenal of Russian obscenities; it comes from the most common Russian obscene word for "penis," which suggests "Putin is a dick" as a possible English equivalent. But its relative rarity demands something a bit more specific, and since it describes someone who is something along the lines of the American insult "asshole," "dickhead" seems appropriate enough.

"Putin—khuilo" turns out to have been almost literally crowdsourced from the very beginning. A variation on a 2010 Ukrainian soccer chant ("Surkis Khuilo"), the new chant easily substitutes the Ukrainian Football Federation president with the Russian president in Kharkiv in March 2014, when even soccer hooligans readily admit that there are more pressing matters than the dispute between rival team-owning Ukrainian oligarchs. The result is a chant that alternates the words "Putin is a dickhead" with a drunken chorus of "la la la."[3]

The chant enjoyed enormous memetic success. A metal remix of the original video spread throughout the Internet, a Ukrainian band called Teleri came out with a song and video called "Putin Hello," a Ukrainian TV station broadcast a live performance of the "Putin khuilo" on May 29, and nine different video versions of the song were eventually reviewed by the Kyiv Post.[4]

Nor have Ukrainian politicians been shy about joining the party. The Radical Party of Oleh Liashko used the phrase on billboards during the 2014 parliamentary electoral campaign.[5] Naturally, the words have appeared as graffiti throughout the former Soviet Union, making the jump to the Internet rather quickly.[6]

We should not be surprised to see a leader insulted with a reference to what the philosopher Mikhail Bakhtin so delicately called "the lower bodily stratum." Calling attention to this particular area of the body is a sure-fire way to strip a victim of dignity. But the nether regions provide more than one option. The round and bald Nikita Khrushchev earned the nickname "ass with ears"; here we have a clear reference to his appearance, but also an implied characterization of him as foolish and flabby.

Perhaps one can make a visual case for Putin's phallic appearance, but that would seem to be a secondary concern. A closer context is the implied aggression of a phallic characterization, one whose appropriateness during an invasion is readily apparent. Recall the old joke about Brezhnev commissioning a sculpture to do a bust of his likeness. Two weeks later, Brezhnev returns to see that his stone representation is equipped with breasts. The sculptor explains that it's an allegory: with one breast, Leonid Ilich feeds the working class; with the other, the peasantry—leaving Brezhnev with the question: "But what about the intelligentsia?" To which the sculptor replies, "Leonid Ilich, it's only a bust."

The joke works, but it is also one of the few occasions on which the senescent Brezhnev is tacitly figured in an active, energetic role. The postmodernist writer Vladimir Sorokin has on more than one occasion framed state executive power in terms of anal sex; in his 1999 novel *Blue Lard*, clones of Stalin and Khrushchev have sex, with Stalin on top.[7] Years later, the climax of his Putinist satire *Day of the Oprichnik* includes an all-male bane "caterpillar orgy" (imagine anal sex as a conga line).[8]

Putin, however, is the anti-Brezhnev. More to the point, he is the anti-Yeltsin. By the end of Yeltsin's reign, the president's image was of an overweight drunk kept alive by the best cardiologists money could buy. If the king has two bodies, does not the president (our modern king) have two penises (by extension, as it were)? Here Kantorowicz's framing of supreme executive power proves positively Lacanian: the individual president may have a penis, but it is the supra-president who has the phallus. And never the twain shall meet. For if they do, the penis undermines the phallus.

"Putin—khuilo" works because it attacks the Russian president using the body part that most clearly exemplifies his public persona, style of leadership, and symbolic repositioning of Russian statehood. While "Putin—khuilo" may be a value judgment, it is not just a negative assessment of the Russian Federation's leader; it is also the inevitable abject, parodic shadow of the president's anatomical destiny: Putin's presidency is phallic through and through.

We are all familiar with the unrelenting masculinity of Putin's image, and it is the rare Western comedian who mentions the Russian president without referring to the famous pictures of him riding shirtless on horseback. It is the particularly phallic emphasis within Putin's masculinity that must be noted here.[9] Putin himself has not hesitated to appropriate explicitly phallic language, suggesting that a reporter who seemed soft on Islam should get circumcised and be careful not to have too much removed. More important, though, is the aforementioned contrast between Putin and his flaccid predecessors, which extends to a more generalized discursive emphasis on all manners of erections. Putin raised the country from its knees. Putin's philosophy of governing is based on the "vertical of power." The phallus is the symbolic penis that is always understood to be erect, but Putin's phallic appeal is as much a matter of process as product: not just having the erection, but achieving it. It is national destiny as the penis's progress. In his 1920 call for building a national power grid, Lenin declared that communism was Soviet power plus the electrification of the entire country.[10] A century later, Putinism equals vertical power plus the viagrification of the entire Russian Federation.

"Obama Is a Shmoe"

This particular viral phenomenon, like "Putin is a Dickhead," migrated back and forth from off-line to online. The symmetry between the two makes sense: the leaders of two of the world's most powerful countries are simply too big, too omnipresent, either to be limited to the Internet or kept off of it. Nor does the symmetry end here, since both insults stress (or undermine) their targets' masculinity. Though there are plenty of etymologies for the Russian word "Chmo" that are based on Russian acronyms, the most likely explanation is that it is a cognate with the English word "shmoe."[11] Both words, then, derive from the Yiddish and are euphemisms for male genitalia. But where "khuilo" (dickhead) suggests erection, the pathetic, ineffective "shmoe" is flaccid and powerless. A dickhead is many things, but he is not impotent.

63

Prior to the "Shmoe" memes, Obama had become firmly associated with one particular phallic object, though for reasons more racist than sexual: again and again, Obama was (and is) depicted holding or eating bananas. As in the United States, much of the hatred for Barak Obama expressed itself in racial terms, but in the absence of a large Black community or a vocal, organized anti-racist consensus, such memes were less likely to be met with immediate condemnation. The banana memes also fit into the frequent portrayal of Obama as an ape, all of which was facilitated by Russian phonetics (not just "Obama" and "banan" (banana) but also the Russian word for ape, "obeziana"). The producers of state television were more than happy to engage in racist dogwhistle about Obama, but one incident did show there was an awareness of possibly crossing a line: when the head of Russians television news operations Dmitry Kiselyov made a reference to Obama and jungles in November 2016, it was cut from later rebroadcasts.[12]

Anti-Obama memes were particularly noteworthy in the aftermath of the annexation of Crimea and the euphoria over the seventieth anniversary of the Soviet victory in the Second World War. As we will see in the next chapter, the anniversary helped turn Russian automobiles into roving meme-delivery vehicles, thanks to the stickers and slogans plastered on their back windshields, and these memes found their way to the Internet as well. "Obama is an Ape" found its way onto bumper stickers, as did even more openly hostile slogans ("Want to buy Obama's skin. Money is no object") ("Kupliu kozhu Obamy dorogo"). And then there was "Obama is a Shmoe," which is short and to the point (only two words and four syllables in Russian).

On the Internet, the static image of "Obama is a Shmoe" was often merely pictures of cars displaying the slogan. The make and condition of the cars could be interpreted as a comment on the person making the declaration: the proliferation of images of "Obama is a Shmoe" on filthy, dilapidated domestic cars turns the insult back on the car owner (see Figure 2).

But "Obama is a Shmoe" also went viral in a series of video recordings of various Russians declaiming, screaming, or singing the phrase as part of what English speakers call a challenge, and Russians

Figure 2 "Obama Is a Shmoe" sticker on a filthy car.

call a flashmob.[13] Several parents posted videos of their small children repeating the phrase; another shows two preteen boys jumping and dancing to their own "Obama is a Shmoe" song. One man recording himself railing against Obama, threatening his life, and shooting a rifle in the forest. Two teenage boys recorded a rap called "Obama is a Shmoe," calling America shit, referring to the president's "monkey face," and wondering who is this "f*ggot" who shoves his "fucking black face" in where it isn't wanted.

The teenage boys demonstrate a curious twist in their attacks on Barack Obama: setting explicitly racist tropes to the beats of rap music, without any sign of cognitive dissonance (the preteen boys perform their anti-Obama chant while dancing, hip-hop style, to DJ Snake's and Lil Jon's "Turn Down the What"). While it is true that white Americans have proven themselves more than capable of appropriating Black culture while oppressing Black people, it is still difficult to disentangle hip-hop from blackness. But Russian hip-hop was white (or at any rate, not Black) from the very beginning. The boys' reference to Obama's "fucking black face" ("chernoe eblo') proves apt: it is precisely Obama's Black physicality, the visual display of his blackness, that not only colors the form of the hostility against him but lends itself to exploitation by the visual language of Internet memes.

Rap provides the idiom for Russian anti-Obama viral video. In 2015, one of the most beloved comedians of the Soviet era, Mikhail

Meanwhile, In Russia

Zadornov, released a three-minute "Obama is a Shmoe" video compiling a brief clip of Obama with a number of unrelated images as he quasi-rapped about the "dark-skinned ruler who'll soon be punished for it all."[14] One of Obama's many crimes is his "slander" against Putin introducing a motif common to many of the "Schmoe" videos: the contrast between the two presidents. Indeed, many anti-Obama memes are as much about Putin as they are about his (former) American counterpart. Putin is strong where Obama is weak, Putin is good where Obama is evil, and, of course, Putin is white where Obama is Black.[15]

Hating Greta

Anti-Obama memes are not unique to Russia; surely, Americans have produced more of them. But Obama is an obvious example of the disparities in both news and meme cultures between Russia and the United States. Thanks in part to the aggressive conservatism and conspiracy-mongering of Russian state television, attitudes and expressions that would, in America, be associated with Fox News and the Alt-Right are closer to the mainstream. The political leanings of a given online community make the reactions to certain public figures rather predictable.

At the heart of one of the last big international media and memetic phenomena before the Covid-19 outbreak was the teenage environmentalist Greta Thunberg. Famous for initiating school strikes for climate in 2018, at the age of fifteen, she took the 2019–20 school year off and sailed to the United States, where, on September 23, she gave a speech at the United Nations Climate Action Summit. Calling for immediate action, she challenged her audience:

> This is all wrong. I shouldn't be up here. I should be back in school on the other side of the ocean. Yet you all come to us young people for hope? *How dare you!* You have stolen my dreams and my childhood with your empty words. [. . .] We are in the beginning of a mass extinction. And all you can talk

about is money and fairy tales of eternal economic growth. How dare you![16]

The mainstream media in the United States and much of Europe loved Greta, but conservatives and climate skeptics found her odious. It is important to note that, beyond the politics of climate change or differing views on youth activism, Greta was such a productive source of memes for other, specifically personal reasons: she is on the autism spectrum. Her manner of speaking and facial expressions deviate from the norm, challenging listeners and viewers who are either uninformed about neurodiversity or unmoved by the idea of making accommodations.

In Russia, people with disabilities have only recently begun claiming their right to be seen and to take up space in public. Traditionally, parents were encouraged to institutionalize children with developmental disabilities in special schools that essentially warehoused them, with little effort made to incorporate them into the mainstream world or educate neurotypical people about the varieties of human experience that include disability. And suddenly, the world is supposed to pay attention to a teenage girl who proudly talks about her autism while displaying no concern about how other people see her. When Russian meme-makers seized on the many images of an angry Greta haranguing her elders, they were doing much the same as their Anglophone counterparts. Furious Greta had a face that was made for memeing.

But Russian meme-makers did their work in a mainstream context that was much more open in its disdain for the Swedish girl's activism. The popular tabloid *Komsomolskaya Pravda* covered her speech with the headline "Mentally Ill Girl Promised Humankind's 'Mass Extinction.'"[17] A commentator on a national newscast referred to her as a "sick girl who is as stupid as she is naive." Her presence on the world stage was an affront: If she could not get her face and voice under control, why should anyone listen to her?

Some of the "Angry Greta" memes deliberately trivialized her outrage: "January has 31 days, but February has 29. You've stolen two days of my childhood, you bastards!"; "Protect nature, motherfuckers!";

"You milk cows, it's inhuman!" One meme, entitled "The emotions of our little Greta, our goddess, our mistress," consists of a grid with twelve different pictures of Greta, each labeled with a different feeling. Ironically, this meme bears a remarkable resemblance to the image boards often given to autistic children to help them read facial expressions. The meme-maker has unwittingly closed the autistic loop.

Like Anglophone right-wing meme-makers, their Russian counterparts frequently reframe Greta as totalitarian. Her angry face gets juxtaposed with that of Hitler, Emperor Palpatine, sometimes photoshopped into images of the Nuremberg rallies. While dismissing progressive activism as the "totalitarian Left" has been going on for decades, the totalitarian trope takes on extra resonance in a country that used to be part of the Soviet Union.

In addition, the allegations that she is merely a puppet in the hands of more wily "villains" (such as George Soros, whose picture with Greta has also made the rounds in Russian memes) have a particularly Soviet prehistory. As the noted opposition figure and blogger Alexei Navalny argues in a video devoted to the Greta phenomenon, Russians who were children during the 1980s have clear memories of little girls' images being used for propaganda purposes.[18] In November 1982, a ten-year-old girl from Maine named Samantha Smith wrote a letter to Soviet primer Yuri Andropov, pleading with him not to start a war with the United States. Her letter was published in Pravda, as was Andropov's response; in short order, Samantha Smith became a global superstar. As a "global ambassador," she visited Russia, where she was celebrated as a peace activist. Her life was cut tragically short due to a plane crash in 1985.

Samantha Smith was not alone, however. Not long after her death, an American foundation called "Children as the Peacemakers" invited the Soviets to send a girl on a goodwill mission to the United States. The girl who was selected, Katya Lycheva, became a Soviet media darling. Navalny explains how sick he and all his friends were of hearing about Katya in school and having to write letters in support of her mission. In her broadside against Greta, the libertarian journalist Yuliya Latynina connects her to what she calls the "Pioneer Girl" type, the crusading schoolgirl whose humorless devotion to the cause makes her the perfect subject of a totalitarian society.[19] Certainly, the Soviet Union was not lacking in famous girl martyrs; generations of schoolchildren were brought up on stories of the heroic teenage partisan Zoya Kosmodemyanskaya, who was tortured and murdered by the Nazis.[20]

Of course, it was not only girls who were deployed as martyrs in Soviet propaganda—anyone who grew up on that part of the world remembers the story of Pavlik Morozov, the thirteen-year-old boy who in 1932 allegedly denounced his own father as an enemy of the state, only to be murdered by other members of his family.[21] It is not surprising that many Russians are skeptical about the very phenomenon of young children displaying as activists of any stripe and assume that they are probably being manipulated by the adults in their lives. Moreover, Greta became a phenomenon after several years during which the Russian state had been using the figure of the innocent, naive child as the justification for a variety of repressive measures, from Internet censorship to anti-LGBT legislation to adoption bans. For all of Putin's third term as president, the state media had been reminding their audience that children have no agency and must be defended at all costs. In this context, Greta was a poor fit.

Take That, Elon Musk!

Obama, Putin, and even Greta Thunberg were inevitable as the subjects of Russian memes, and the course taken by each set of memes and videos was not particularly surprising. Anyone following the Russian-language media could have predicted the memes' general attitude, if not their specific forms. "Dickhead" might not have been guaranteed but irreverent anti-Putinism was.

Some of the best Internet memes, however, are thoroughly contingent. "Sad Keanu" took the Internet by storm not because we expect Keanu Reeves to be sad but because of a particular photograph that lent itself to this meme.[22] Sad Keanu is a permanent resident of Russia's MemeWorld, which makes sense because both the image and the actor are very well known beyond America's borders. Nor is this the only macro featuring

Reeves; the Russian Internet features the same standard complement of Keanu memes as can be found on the Anglophone web. Apparently, no matter where he is, Keanu is Keanu is Keanu.

In other cases, two different meme cultures "share" a celebrity but put them to diverging uses. Such is the case of Elon Musk. Born in South Africa, Musk made a name for himself in the United States as a wealthy inventor, engineer, and entrepreneur. He is the force behind the Tesla, Neuralink, SpaceX, and the Hyperloop and is either a visionary, eccentric, or both, depending on one's vantage point: he is passionate about establishing a colony on Mars and made headlines in 2020 by naming his son "X Æ A-12" (which eventually became "X AE A-XII")

Musk is also quite media savvy and self-aware, meeting Tony Stark for lunch in *Iron Man 2*, playing himself on *The Simpsons*, *South Park*, and *Rick and Morty*, and even cohosting PewDiePie's Meme Review on YouTube in February 2019 with *Rick and Morty* cocreator Justin Rolland (apparently at the request of PewDiePie's fans). Compared to Jeff Bezos or the dead-eyed Mark Zuckerberg, Musk comes off as a tech plutocrat you might want to have a beer with. Or maybe not just a beer. One popular Musk meme comes from his 2018 appearance on the Joe Rogan Experience podcast, when he puffed on a cannabis-laced cigar.

The smoking meme was also popular in Russia, showing a contemplative Musk semi-grimacing while holding the infamous cigar. Like the English memes, they suggest that some of Musk's wilder ideas are the stuff of weed-induced reveries: "Let's make a flying table?" "Why don't we shoot Earth into space?," as well as the caption "Elon Musk has found a new way to get to Mars." A photo of Musk dancing with what looks like a mariachi band also made its way into Russian memes, nor are these the only Russian memes made with Musk's image.

The Russian meme-makers diverge, however, by making an entirely counterintuitive move: the most productive Elon Musk meme format doesn't show Musk at all. Rather, they show objects and moments from contemporary Russian life accompanied by a challenge: "What do you think of that, Elon Musk?"

What, exactly, do these memes show? We might call them post-Soviet life hacks: ridiculous yet occasionally ingenious ways of repurposing ordinary objects to meet a need. For instance, a light bulb held in place with a Kryptonite lock, a makeshift ladle formed from a fork and a plastic cup, a TV ceiling mount made out of plastic coat hangers, or a windshield wiper replaced with the traditional Russian *vennik* (a short-handled broom made out of twigs and other plant materials; the English equivalent is called a "besom"). Perhaps unsurprisingly, a number of them have to do with alcohol: using a Jack Daniels bottle to replace the missing leg of a chair or stacking empty beer bottles to make a table.

Behind these memes is a particular combination of self-deprecation and pride: yes, things might not work as smoothly here, but we make the best of things thanks to our unfailing ingenuity. That Elon Musk, invisible in nearly all these memes, serves as a yardstick makes a fair amount of sense.

Musk's international reputation is that of a genius, and Russians are taught to pride themselves for living in a country that has produced more than its fair share.[23] But the history of Russian ingenuity is, as often as not, a story of brilliant inventors stymied by a political and/or economic system that is not conducive to bringing their ideas to fruition. Emigration from the Soviet Union, starting in the 1970s, facilitated a "brain drain" of some of the best and the brightest. This has continued to be the case even in the post-Soviet era, particularly when it comes to the Internet. Look no further than journalist Andrei Loshchack's excellent seven-part documentary series "Internyet: A History of the Russian Internet" (in Russian with English subtitles).[24] Loshchack interview all the surviving movers and shakers of the Russian online commerce, social media, and digital news, and after a few episodes one cannot help but notice: most of the interview subjects no longer live in Russia.

Musk, however, is not an Internet entrepreneur, despite his obvious comfort with the world of Twitter and YouTube. One of his most notable companies is also one of his most visible endeavors represented in Russian MemeWorld: SpaceX, a privately owned manufacturer of rockets and aerospace technology in the service of Musk's dream of a human colony on Mars. After the successful launch of SpaceX's FalconHeavy rocket in 2018, First Deputy Prime Minister Igor Shuvalov told a group of finalists in the "Russia's Leaders" competition, "I am sure that Russians are a more talented people than the Americans."[25] This quote soon became part of a widely shared "What do you think of that, Elon Musk?" meme, depicting a shirtless Russian man wearing a toilet seat around his neck and using the seat back to hold a large (nearly empty) bottle of beer (see Figure 3).

In the United States, the FalconHeavy launch was yet another reminder of how far we've come from NASA's heyday; the astronauts with the proverbial "right stuff" could hardly have imagined that in just a few short decades, the future of space exploration would be in the hands of a billionaire tech bro. But this was a much more significant blow to Russian prestige than American; Russia, as the successor to the Soviet Union, still basks in the glory of having sent the first man (and the first woman) into space. The Cosmonauts featured prominently in the Soviet media and state propaganda as a symbol of the triumph of the Soviet system and the death knell of superstition. Yuri Gagarin, the first man in space, was reportedly to have said, "I looked and looked and looked, but I didn't see God," while a famous propaganda poster put it more plainly: a drawing of a cosmonaut floating in space

Шувалов ответил на запуск ракеты SpaceX словами «русский народ более талантлив»

КАК ТЕБЕ ТАКОЕ, ИЛОН МАСК?

Figure 3 "Shuvalov responded to the SpaceX launch with the words 'The Russian people are more talented.' Take That, Elon Musk!"

hovered over the slogan "There is no God!"[26] The official atheism is gone, but the national pride remains.

By privatizing space exploration, Musk is not just competing with (former) superpowers; he is symbolically taking the place of the people who dethroned God. This is, of course, hyperbole, but not unjustified: the space program was the culmination of a Soviet Promethean impulse, a socialist humanism that saw all of nature as subject to control and even conquest by rational science. Shuvalov's need to defend his people's ingenuity in the face of Musk's success is a typically blunt, self-serious response, one which the meme-makers turn into the stuff of gentle irony turned against both self and other.

The self-deprecating pride shown in the Musk memes' absurd Russian life hacks shows how differently this kind of humor is received when it is produced within the country that is the butt of the joke. Just two decades before SpaceX, the Russian parliament expressed its outrage at the depiction of a cosmonaut in the 1998 Jerry Bruckheimer film *Armageddon*.[27] Inexplicably clad in a Russian fur hat, drunken cosmonaut Lev Andropov maintains the dilapidated Mir space station with roughly the same sort of ingenuity displayed in the Musk memes.

As is often the case, analyzing these often funny memes threatens to kill the humor and that would be a particular shame in this case. The Elon Musk memes address a serious set of issues by deliberately not taking them so seriously. In an atmosphere of increasingly militarized rhetoric regarding Russia's relations with the outside world, someone posted this meme of a door propped open by a plastic bag affixed to the wall:

The door to the cafeteria in our loser college [sharaga] is held open LIKE THIS. So, elon musk, are you feeling the threat?

In these memes, Elon Musk is the absent judge of all things Russian, summoned in the form of a brazen challenge: What do you think of that? These memes rely on the foreign gaze that so often haunts Russian culture, a gaze that does not have to be real to be effective. As in Foucault's panopticon, the prison structure in which every inmate knows he could be watched but does not know for sure when he is being watched, the foreign gaze becomes internalized. ("How is the West looking at us? Are they looking at us?") These memes acknowledge (and even invoke) the foreign gaze while also laughing at it, at the same time mocking the hypothetical Russian subject that keeps assuming it is being looked at.

If only all cold wars were this cool.

CHAPTER 6
THE WHOLE WORLD IS WATCHING

In Soviet Russia

In the prologue to Dmitri Kolodan's *Maskarad. Zerkala (1)*
(*Masquerade. Mirrors, Book One*), a 2012 novel in the best-selling
young adult "Ethnogenesis" series, aspiring Russian actress Tomka
Koshkina has just arrived in Venice, only to fall victim to a series of
practical jokes at the hands of her new Italian acquaintances, Gepetto
and Laura. The Italians act as though they know her and soon reveal
their shock that Tomka is unaware that she is an international celebrity:

> "Well, you know," said Gepetto carefully. "You're that—"
>
> "Crazy Russian Girl on Stilts," Laura finished for him. We've
> watched your clip on YouTube a thousand and one times."
> (Kolodan, prologue)

Without her knowledge, someone had uploaded a video of Tomka
practicing for the upcoming Venice carnival, and now Tomka finds she
is a hero of worldwide slapstick, with offers from the Cirque du Soleil.
Tomka's Internet misadventures are only a minor incident in a sixty-
volume saga that spans all space and time, but her inadvertent fame
is instructive. After flying across a continent to arrive in Venice, she
discovers that her own digital image has beat her to her destination,
hobbling on stilts and pixels over borders and T1 lines. Reputation,
it turns out, travels at light speed, while mere mortals must make do
with more conventional transport.

Tomka's celebrity would be immediately legible to the *Ethnogenesis*
fans who encounter it; only her ignorance comes off as disconcerting.

After all, viral content has become an integral part of the Russian mediascape. Unlike pre-digital examples of Russian popular performance (such as that of pop diva, Alla Pugacheva), Russian viral video crosses geographic and cultural borders with unprecedented ease. netizens in the West have mined Russia's online digital archives as a reliable source of the profoundly weird, from dashboard camera recordings of wayward trucks spilling cattle onto highways to the (re) discovery of Eduard Khil's 1976 unintentionally hilarious "Vocalise" ("The Trololo Man").[1] Taken together, such memes and viral videos create a virtual Russia that, while by no means coextensive with the real country or even its culture, throw the landmarks of the discourse of Russia and Russianness into sharp relief.

When viewed in the context of Russian cultural history, Russian viral content plays a paradoxical role on the world stage. On the one hand, Russia's prominence could be seen as a partial remedy for wounded cultural pride. Going back at least as far as the late eighteenth century, the country's habit of borrowing cultural forms from Europe not only prompted intermittent anxiety about a loss of a notional, primordial "Russianness"; but also threatened to turn the country into a net importer of culture rather than an exporter. To put things simplistically, nineteenth-century Russian literature partly rectified the problem, as did Russian classical music. In the early twentieth century, the Russian avant-garde was also prominent on the world scene; and after that, there was always, well, communism.

But whatever appeal communism might have had as an export, within the Soviet Union, the threat of the growing American superculture loomed large (especially after the Second World War). By the time the USSR ceased to exist in 1991, Soviet and post-Soviet Russian culture was particularly vulnerable. The film and television industry all but collapsed, while the less said about most of 1990s Russian pop music, the better. In the three decades since 1991, the occasional Russian cultural product has found resonance abroad (T.A.T.U, Metro 2033, Pussy Riot), but the greatest success story has been Russian memes.

As a success, it is nonetheless bittersweet. The key to the broader appeal of Russian memes is far removed from any discourse of

Russian greatness. Instead, it plays into just the sort of stereotypes that, in other contexts, have caused public expressions of outrage. The Russia represented in the memes and viral video consumed by outsiders is a wacky land of angry drunks, shoddy workmanship, antiquated technology, and out of control drivers. It is a Disneyland of dysfunction (though, ironically enough, without the long lines).[2]

Many Russians have been understandably upset by these stereotypes. In America, they have a long history, often associated with the joke format known as the "Russian Reversal." The earliest known example is from a 1938 Cole Porter song, followed by a Bob Hope performance at the 1958 Oscars. It would rise to prominence through its association with the hokey Soviet émigré comedian Yakov Smirnov, who, in addition to his well-known catchphrase "What a country!," used the format on occasion. The Russian Reversal, if we paraphrase Bob Hope's use of it, boils down to a two-part statement, such as "In America, you watch TV. In Soviet Russia, TV watches you!" [3]

Initially predicated on the contrast between the "free" United States and "totalitarian" Soviet Union, the Russian Reversal has expanded to include contrast based on a predictable or rational America and a chaotic, inexplicable Russia. The phrase "in Soviet Russia" is one that no Russian speaker would ever use; while the Soviet Union existed, it was only outsiders who used the name interchangeably with Russia; within the USSR, it would have been like passing off New York for America. After 1991, the phrase makes even less sense: whatever one calls the successor states to the USSR (in this case, the Russian Federation), they are not "Soviet." Never a very clear term to Americans during the Cold War, "Soviet" now seems to mean "anything to do with Russia, particularly if it's weird."

When Russian memes are curated for an English-language audience, "In Soviet Russia" is a common rubric that immediately contextualizes the material for its potential viewers. The other is "Meanwhile in Russia," the phrase that forms the title of the present study. Know Your Meme connect the "Meanwhile in X" image macro with a common saying that dates back to American silent movies about cowboys: "Meanwhile, back at the ranch . . ." Initially an intertitle alerting the audience to a change in scenery, it has long since become a sarcastic response to a conversation that has veered far off topic. The first attested "Meanwhile in X" meme dates back to February 2010, when the words "Meanwhile in Australia" were superimposed over the upside-down image of an Australian car (since Australia is "upside down" from the point of view of someone in the Northern Hemisphere).[4] Though the "upside down" feature only technically applies to this first meme, it is nonetheless an excellent metaphor for the entire "Meanwhile in X" memetic constellation: "Meanwhile" memes are dispatches from a world where up is down, and where people behave in ways that don't make sense to the imagined "normal" viewer.

As the algebraic formulation in "Meanwhile in X" suggest, Russia does not have any exclusive claim to this sort of meme. But Russia has been an extremely reliable source of material, keeping the memes flowing at a steady pace. While there are any number of sociocultural factors that could explain certain individual memes, or the prevalence of a particular type of meme protagonists, the country's high alcoholism rates, for example, would explain why so many of the memes feature drunks. But the main culprit is to be found at the nexus of public policy, corruption, and technology: the rise of the dashboard camera or dashcam.

Russian Road Rage

When installed in a motor vehicle, the dashcam provides continuous, automatic recording, usually of whatever can be seen through the front windshield. They also record sound. The technology is available worldwide, though local laws may vary. The Russian government removed any obstacle to their distribution in 2009, whereupon sales skyrocketed.[5] Dashcams are a hedge against the notorious corruption of the traffic police, as well as liability scams. By 2014, dashcams had become ubiquitous, with over a million vehicles equipped with the recording device.[6] By that point, dashcam recordings of strange or amusing events were equally ubiquitous on YouTube, whether as "fails" for Channels such as FailArmy or through sites and social media pages such as Meanwhile in Russia and In Soviet Russia. Before

2013, knowledge of Russian dashcam videos in the West could serve as an indicator of exactly how "online" a given Internet user actually was. To primarily younger Netizens, Russian dashcams were a staple of the Internet, part of a handful of virtual phenomena that became identified with Russians. Russians were also the butt of jokes on gaming sites and Twitch, both for their occasionally weak English and their prolific swearing (by now, what gamer doesn't know the words the words "suka" and "bliad'" [sometimes spelled "blyat"])?

Dashcam video reached the big time in the West on February 15, 2013, when a meteor landed just outside of Chelyabinsk (Siberia). Since then, dashcam videos of street fights and overturned trucks spilling cattle onto the road have become a staple of viral video (particularly after Jon Stewart aired a compilation just five days after the meteor strike). Here Stewart deliberately treats the freakish recorded events as if they were everyday occurrences: "They've long been accustomed to the fact that your average Russian car can easily be torn apart by your average Russian woman." Two drivers confronting each other with a baseball bat is called a "typical roadside scene." He concludes, "Russia is like a live-action version of Grant Theft Auto."[7] The point here is not to take Stewart to task for exaggeration (exaggeration is his stock and trade) but, rather, to note the way in which viral video is used to perform an idea of Russia that takes preexisting notions of national character and expands their boundaries further. Dashcam videos had been available on YouTube for years before Stewart's compilation aired, but the meteor strike functioned as a particularly dramatic "pointer" to the Russian Federation: now that an astronomical catastrophe has got our attention, let us see what else we can find in the neighborhood. The world's attention returns to Russia when the nation's airspace is disrupted by the celestial equivalent of a stray bullet; the dashcam recordings of the event in turn draw attention both to the dashcam phenomenon and to the Russian roads themselves.

The inaccuracy of Stewart's description of the "typical roadside scene" does more than reinforce Russian stereotypes; it also deliberately distorts the very nature of dashcam video. By design, the dashcam provides a never-ending supply of recordings from the Russian road; they are on by default. The overwhelming majority of this video has to be mind-numbingly boring. Dashcam videos that make it to the Internet are *curated*; if they weren't in some way unusual, who would bother to upload them? If there is an audience for hours of recordings in which cars come to a full stop at red lights, drivers follow the rules of the road, and livestock fails to spill from moving vehicles, chances are good that it is a niche phenomenon. When Russian drivers post these videos, they are identifying these events as freakish, or at least worthy of attention; but are they identifying these scenes as uniquely Russian? In some cases, based on comments, almost certainly, there is a long-standing tradition of taking an almost perverse pride in idiosyncratic national dysfunction (or in the perception thereof). But in an entirely Russian context, they could just be simply funny videos, full stop. It is when they travel to the wider Internet that they are inevitably tagged as Russian.

What might be more specifically Russian is not the content of the Russian road videos, but the outsize roles of the roads themselves and of motor vehicles. Private car ownership was rare in Soviet times, thanks to both the ubiquity of mass transit and the shortage of automobiles. In the post-Soviet years, public transportation is still extensive, but the roads are now filled with cars of all makes and models, with endless traffic jams in the big cities rendering car ownership a somewhat masochist luxury. In Moscow alone, car ownership jumped from 60 automobiles per 1,000 residents in 1991 to 350 in 2009.[8] In years when activism was fairly muted, issues related to driving and roads galvanized otherwise apolitical citizens. In addition to having a strong social media presence, "automobilists" have frequently organized to advocate for their own corporate interests. Their challenges to local and federal authorities manage to be political in the broadest sense (i.e., concerned with the well-being of the citizenry) without necessarily being political in the narrower (and more fraught) sense.[9] Whether protesting tax hikes on car ownership, agitating against the abuse of VIP flashing lights by placing blue sand buckets upside down on their cars' hoods, or expressing outrage over the frequency with which the rich and well-connected can get away with vehicular manslaughter.

The ubiquity of the dashcam is the most visible sign that, in Russia, Internet culture and car culture have strong connections that precede any discussion of smart-cars or self-driving vehicles. In the Introduction, I argued for the significance of the compressed post-Soviet time frame that brought commercial advertising and market-based entertainment only a few years before the rise of the Runet and Internet memes. While cars obviously predate the Soviet collapse, mass automobile ownership is part of that same compressed time frame. As a network, the Internet shares a number of common features with the older networks that are the hallmarks of an industrialized society: electricity (whose extension to the entire population was the great Soviet success story of the 1920s), telephones (less of a success story in the Soviet Union), heat, water, radio, television, and, of course, mass transit. The decline of many such networks is a defining feature of neoliberal Russia, as they are supplanted by private, individual-based solutions allowing the better off to opt out of failing public systems (such as medicine and education).[10] Car ownership, as an alternative to mass transit, is yet another symptom.

But car ownership also produces new meanings. Soviet drivers did not take part in North America's tradition of affixing bumper stickers with slogans, sayings, or images to their vehicles. To be clear: neither did most of the rest of the world, but the Soviet context would have made such a practice unworkable: either the messages would have been the same state-approved propaganda seen on banners and posters (in which case, what's the point?), or they would have been an invitation to unwanted scrutiny. In the post-Soviet era, cars became one of the many new sites of self-expression that popped up under the new political conditions, in a development that paralleled both the country's economic transformation (from state ownership to privatization), the eventual fate of media in the Internet era (from the central newspaper to the "Daily Me"), and the transformation of public space (from the public "wall newspaper" to the individual car sticker). The cars provided a whiteboard on which car owners could express either random, amusing thoughts or political statements that fall within the range of the acceptable.

A 2016 article in *Novaia gazeta* catalogues some of the more noteworthy examples of the genre, from the sentimental ("My love! Thank you for giving me a son!") to the aggressively sarcastic ("Go ahead and try to pass me! Someone needs your kidneys") to the random ("Space Alien Deportation Dept.").[11] But there was also room for politics and patriotism, particularly after Russia's annexation of Crimea: "Russia is our holy state"; "The Russian army is the strongest in the world." One sticker had an image of Putin side by side with Stalin (which could be either good or bad, depending on the driver's world view), while another said, "Putin, get out." At the time, one also could see anti-Obama slogans and images, often comparing him to a monkey.

Cars became vehicles (sorry) for militaristic patriotism around the seventieth anniversary of the Soviet victory in Second World War. Long a (justifiable) source of national pride, the defeat of Germany took on additional resonance this time around. State propaganda had spent the previous year insisting that the supporters of Ukrainian independence were the heirs of notorious Nazi collaborators, casting the conflict in Ukraine as a reenactment of the Soviet fight against fascism. The political mobilization of the Russian populace became literal, with the intensification of the Immortal Regiment marches that had begun just a few years earlier. But commemoration was not just a pedestrian affair; car owners used their automobiles to display their solidarity with a nation of victors. The tone of many of the stickers affixed to these cars was often aggressive, using history to make a statement about the current state of the world. In addition to the traditional Second World War-era slogan "Onward to Berlin!," variations on "We can do it again!" (i.e., defeat the enemy) were common, sometimes accompanied by stick figures of a Soviet-flag-themed man anally raping a Nazi figure and a Russian-flag themed man doing the same to a man drawn in the colors of the American flag.

Thus cars move messages at the same time as they move people. With the advent of the dashcam, the automotive circulation of information has taken the extra step of serving as a physical extension of the Internet into the everyday world: the Internet of Cars. Even before the dashcam, the ubiquity of surveillance cameras ensured the production of video recordings whose sheer volume (not to mention general tediousness) is such that the world's population could spend all their waking hours watching it and still not exhaust the supply. Surveillance cameras are relatively static: they wait for the world to come to them. The dashcam -equipped automobile puts the engine in search engine. When Russian literary scholars talk about how plots work, the term they use for the conflicts facing the character is "kolliziia"—literally, collision. Dashcam record collisions in both the Russian and English senses as they go out into the world in much the same way individuals do: according to idiosyncratic, often unpredictable routes. The driver of a car is already functionally a part-time cyborg. Successful drivers, when they get behind the wheel, extend their proprioception—their sense of their body's position in space—to the vehicle that they are controlling. The dashcam makes this cyborg the part of a chaotic network, a roving collector of data.

The link between the dashcam and the Internet meme is, of course, curation. Virtually all of the recorded material would be of interest to no one. It is the consciousness of the car owner that registers (i.e., records) the event that is meme-worthy. Before it reaches the West as a possible variation on Russian-themed minstrelsy, the recordings are made available thanks to the judgment, tastes, and prejudices of the presumably Russian driver. The driver behind the wheel may or may not feel a sense of kinship with the subject of the video, but, except in moments when the driver or the driver's car is directly involved, the driver is already in the position of viewer, with the windshield serving as both barrier and screen. The person recorded, whether they are taking an axe to someone else's car, or transporting cattle in a small back seat, is easily framed as an Other: they are crazy, low-class, or simply tacky. This does not mean identification between driver and subjects is not possible; a world-weary resignation about "us Russians" is easy enough to imagine. Only when the meme moves outside the Runet does the subject become completely exoticized.

With that in mind, let us return to Stewart's compilation of "typical" Russian roadside scenes. What immediately becomes striking is the contrast between two different styles of curation, or perhaps two different cultural systems for making sense of dashcam material. Where Stewart gets a lot of mileage out of his phlegmatic Russian subjects' apparent non-reactions to the arrival of several tons of rock from space, the Russian hashtag system on the Livejournal Ru.Chp page, among the many features it highlights, distinguishes between "bricks" (i.e., videos where a horrified driver is "shitting bricks") and "sphincter of steel" (literally, "anus of concrete"), where the driver's response to a brush with death is the verbal equivalent of a shrug.[12] After his report on the meteor, Stewart screens a compilation of dashcam videos to the tune of "Yackety Yack," a classic tool in the Anglo-American audiovisual repertoire of mockery. The clips fall into two categories: Russians engaged in fighting and drunken foolishness, or Russian roads disrupted by unlikely forms of transportation (tanks, fighter jets, fighter choppers). Ru_Chp has hashtags that ironically emphasize Russianness ("How I love my country"), but they are used sparingly. When framed for a Western audience, Russian roads are the arteries through which Russian weirdness circulates.

Squatting Slavs

Foreign representations of Russians often fall into familiar categories (drunks, Mafiosi, and spies immediately come to mind). To go beyond the stereotypes requires curiosity, which has generally been in short supply. But one Russian subcultural archetype has slipped past the new Iron Curtain of Indifference, even making appearances on the runways of Paris and Milan. He is best known in the West as an Internet meme: the squatting Slav. The squatting Slav is usually male, usually young, and usually dressed in cheap streetwear (tracksuits, jeans), often with a cigarette in his hand or dangling from his lower lip. In his natural habitat, he tends to squat on the street, on the top of low walls—in any urban space where chairs are unlikely to be found. On the Internet, he is photoshopped against every conceivable backdrop, from the halls of power to galaxies far, far away.[13] Yet most of the squatting Slav memes lack the inventiveness of the other memes we've examined thus far, because the presence of the squatting Slav is self-sufficient. He does not have to be matched with an amusing slogan (though he can be) or have a movie star's head photoshopped onto his (though it happens—

one meme turns Scully and Mulder from the X-Files into track-suited thugs). Just by squatting, he becomes a meme.

When it circulates abroad, the squatting Slav meme is exotic and devoid of context. While the meme is a source of humor within Russia, squatting itself is less marked than in, say, America, where virtually no one squats unless it is part of a gym regimen. In Russia and the former Soviet Union, sitting on the ground is frowned upon as unhygienic. Schoolchildren do not sit on the floor "criss-cross, apple sauce"; if they have to sit without a chair, they squat. In Russia, it is not the mere fact of squatting that marks the squatting Slav; it is where he squats, the persistence of squatting, what else he is doing and how he is dressed while he is doing it. Externally, the squatting Slav stands in for an entire nation or set of nations; within Russia, he squats at the nexus of stigmatized social class and fears about young low-class men as perpetrators of violent crime. He is a yokel, but he is a dangerous yokel. In Russian, he is called a gopnik.

The word "gopnik" has several conflicting origin stories. One version traces the term back to nineteenth-century slang for sleeping on the street (gopat'); a more popular etymology suggests the term's origins in the acronym "Gorodskoe obshchestvo prizreniia," a shelter for homeless youth in St. Petersburg before the revolution, renamed "Gosduarstvennoe obshchezhite proletariat" after 1917 and preserving both the location and the acronym. It is often connected to the slang "Gop-stop" (mugging), but it is unclear which came first, gop-stop or the gopnik.[14]

The gopnik is marked both visually and verbally. Much of his speech amounts to excessive use of common conversational idioms ("ty chyo?") and veiled threats. The classic scenario is for a gopnik to ask a passerby for money, and if the response is no, the gopnik asks, "A esli naidu?" ("And what if I find some?," a gambit along the lines of "Maybe this'll jog your memory.") The idea of the gopnik has been around since at least the early twentieth century, but it makes sense that he should have his moment after 1991. A sharp increase in actual crime was accompanied by a far more precipitous growth in the representation of crime in the media, film, and fiction. Crime exerted an irresistible fascination at the same time that it occasioned serious anxiety and intermittent moral panics. But gopniki were not mafia bosses or serial killers; in a new world of vast criminal networks, the gopniki were barely organized crime. As folk devils go, they were rather petty demons.[15]

If the gopnik's broader Internet fame results from his eye-catching stance, this is not entirely a case of foreigners distorting something they do not understand. In Russia, the gopnik is a collection of stereotypical traits, from his clothes to his hair to his manner of speaking, but squatting is nonetheless central to the gopnik image. Once again, we are dealing with a small subgroup exaggerating something that is present throughout the country (on its own, squatting is not particularly unusual in Russia). The squatting gopnik is a precariously balanced compromise between the gopnik as frightening social blight and the gopnik as figure of fun. The position is hardly dignified, but its prevalence in Russian prison camps (which are not known for making comfortable public seating a priority) lends an air of menace.

The humor of the "squatting Slav" meme often involves assuming the position in unlikely places against ridiculous backdrops, but the gopnik's squat has a particular spatial context. The deployment of bodies in public space is a tacit statement of belonging and even ownership. The *babushki* (old women) sit on benches outside of apartment buildings and thereby affirm their right to be there, as well as their function as self-appointed guardians of public behavior. Gopniki squat in public presumably because there is no place to sit; in doing so, they appropriate public space as their own.[16] If babushki are sedentary sentinels, then gopniki are modern-day gargoyles, perching on their heels and as they form a threatening gauntlet for passers-by.

A variation on the common people as uneducated savages, gopniki are only minimally effective as a source of fear. Any such power they have depends on physical presence. Intimidating in "real life," they become ridiculous when transformed into an image. Distance renders the gopnik a figure of fun. In 2010, the TNT national television channel began broadcasting a scripted parody of reality television featuring gopniki in a provincial town: *Real'nye patsany* ("Real Guys"), a hit that is still going, 10 years and more than 200 episodes later.[17] The squatting Slav meme starts to take off in 2012, while the very next year,

Sergei Petrov and a group of like-minded humorists begin publishing two occasional magazines about the gopniki: *Goporez* and *Bratish*. A compendium of squatting Slav photos, straight-faced analyses of gopnik slang, and advice on how to be a gopnik, *Goporez* makes it impossible to take gopniki seriously. Around 2016, street-fashion guru Gosha Rubchinksy releases a collection of gopnik-inspired fashion.

As individuals or groups of actual people, gopniki have been domesticated. As an unindividuated category ("gopota"—"gopnikness" or "the gopnik masses"), they still serve as a rhetorical weapon in public debates about politics. Starting in 2008, critics within the anti-Putin opposition have come to refer to the nationalist masses as the "likuiushchaia gopota" (the triumphant gopnik masses). Gopnik style has conquered the runaway; the squatting Slav has a comfortable home on the Internet, but the "triumphant gopnik masses" still point to an elite discomfort with the ordinary citizens of the Russian Federation who seem ready to support any backward-looking policy.

CHAPTER 7
DANCE DANCE REVOLUTION

If I Can't Dance, I Don't Want to Be Part of Your Viral Video

Long before the creators of most of the memes in this book were born, an American movie musical inadvertently set the pattern for the particular type of moral panic that viral videos would spark in Russia. *Footloose* (1984) starred future meme Kevin Bacon as Ren McCormack, a Chicago teenager who moves to a small town in Oklahoma, only to discover that all forms of dancing and rock music are illegal. Naturally, he cannot let this injustice stand. Fighting for his God-given right to party, he mobilizes his fellow teens to hold a high school prom, despite resistance from the city council and a censorious local reverend. Of course, Ren wins. It's not just that Hollywood films must have happy endings; *Footloose* is an early example of American cinema's insistence that the forces of fun must always win the day, whether the opponent is religion, out-of-touch adults, or high culture.[1] Like the proverbial Chekhov's gun, which must go off by the end of the play if it appears in the beginning, any stuffed-shirt classical musician, opera singer, or religious figure who appears early on in this sort of comedy will inevitably be grooving to the beat before the credits roll.[2]

In addition to all the many more serious things that could be said about it, when it came to popular youth culture, the Soviet Union looked like a production of *Footloose* dragged out over seventy years. From campaigns against the Fox Trot and Jazz in the 1920s, hipsters in the 1950s, Western rock music in the 1960s, unofficial Soviet rock in the 1970s and 1980s, the guardians of Soviet morality were at great pains to police the boundaries of fun. But each of these campaigns, like the struggle to keep Kevin Bacon from busting a move, was doomed to failure. They share a flaw with the Internet's famous Streisand Effect.

Meanwhile, In Russia

Negative attention is still attention, and there is no guarantee that new audiences will share the critics' judgment.

The role that criticism played in disseminating the very phenomena targeted for opprobrium was not as clear in Soviet times, when the state's monopoly on information was, if not total, certainly hegemonic. It took years for jazz to lose its stigma in the Soviet Union; now the time scale is different. With the Internet, audiences can immediately and visibly seize control of the narrative and have an effect on the state media's representation of the issue in real time.

Equally important is that, despite nearly a decade of campaigns for traditional moral values, the Russian public again and again draws the line when it comes to fun.

Twerking Class Heroes

While I am tempted to paraphrase Marx and Engels and assert that a specter is haunting Russia, "haunting" does not usually call up image of thrusting hips and shaking buttocks. This specter, of course, is twerking.

Twerking has not been without controversy in the United States; recall Miley Cyrus's performance with Robin Thicke at the MTV Video Music Awards in 2013. But Russia had a sudden run of twerking controversies all in the course of a single year, 2015. And all of them were facilitated by the Internet.

The first was a video from a concert at an Orenburg dance school. The dance was based on Winnie the Pooh, who is, if anything, even more beloved in the post-Soviet space than he is in the Anglo-American world. In story, Pooh's well-known obsession with honey leads to a conflict with bees, and this particular dance was bee-themed. It begins with someone in a full-body Winnie the Pooh costume standing on stage, holding an empty honey jar, when he is suddenly surrounded by a group of teenage girls dressed in orange and black bee costumes, complete with miniskirts and bare legs. The bees soon turn their backs to the audience and immediately start twerking (as bees do).

The clip went viral, garnering eight million views over one weekend. Children's Ombudsman Pavel Astakhov declared the video "disgusting," while the mayor of Orenburg posted a plea on his website for parents to sign their girls up for "respectable ethnic dances . . . they are the ones that need to be taught," adding, "We live on this land and we need to dance our national dances." Russia's Investigative Committee announced an investigation on charges of "lascivious actions" that could have ended with a fifteen-year prison sentence for the parties deemed responsible. The girls' parents protested, saying that they had given their daughters permission to take the twerking class.

All of this would look like a fairly standard conservative reaction to sexually provocative dancing, were it not for the particular political spin the dance was given by some critics. This was, after all, 2015, when emotions about the war in Ukraine were at their height. Supporters of Russian state policy had adopted the St. George's Ribbon, an old military symbol, as a sign of national pride, while liberals in Russia and foes of Eastern Ukrainian separatism came to see it as a mark of chauvinism. The ribbon is black and orange, like the girls' costumes. The choice of colors could easily be chalked up to coincidence, as bees have been orange and black for a lot longer than the St. George's Ribbon has. But this was a politically paranoid moment. The national daily *Komsomolskaya Pravda* claimed that the costumes "very much resemble the St. George ribbon, and not bees at all." Even if that were the case, it would be difficult to turn the dance into a coherent statement. Does Winnie the Pooh with his empty honey pot represent an undernourished Russia, distracted from its search for food by a group of sexually provocative St. George's Ribbons? If that's the best the opposition can throw at the regime, then Putin can rest comfortably.

The attempt to characterize the Winnie the Pooh dance as an anti-Russian allegory based on a supposed resemblance to a national symbol is worth dwelling on, if only because we see at work not simply a meme but an interpretive strategy. Memes thrive on irreverence, ambiguity, absurdity, and humor; when they are not pointedly political, the interpreter runs the risk of looking obtuse. In this particular case, the interpretation is not, technically, about the meme itself but about the content that was recorded and subsequently turned into a viral video. Presumably, then, whatever malign intent is being imagined here is imputed not to the uploaders but to the choreographers and costume designers. In which case, the dance's anti-patriotic agenda becomes even more dubious: a sinister cabal at a dance school in a town on the border with Kazakhstan dupes naive girls into making an anti-Russian statement in order to . . . corrupt a small group of parents at a concert in Orenburg? The legal case was quickly dropped, but the damage the "patriots" did to their own cause was already done: the attempt to politicize youthful fun looked laughable.

The Twerk of Mourning

The Orenburg twerking teens video was "found" video, a live performance that was captured, remediated, and turned into an Internet phenomenon.[3] The next two twerking scandals that quickly followed involved dances that were performed to be posted on social media, and their political resonance was less the result of interpretive overreach on the part of the viewers than youthful cluelessness on the part of the viewed.

Not long after the bee girl saga, six girls twerked against the backdrop of the Malaya Zemlya Second World War monument in Novorossiisk and uploaded the video, resulting in fines for two of the girls and for the mother of an underaged participant (for "failure to encourage the physical, intellectual, physiological, spiritual, and moral development of a child" "3 Young Women"), and between ten and fifteen days in prison for three of them (the charge: "petty hooliganism"). That September, another set of girls uploaded a video of themselves twerking in front of a war memorial in the Bryansk region, again leading to jail time and fines. The father of one of the girls was forced to transfer out of the Bryansk military base as a result of the scandal.

The timing of these two incidents could not have been worse. Twerking was already in the news thanks to Orenburg, and the country was gearing up for the celebration of the seventieth anniversary of the

Soviet victory over Nazi Germany in an atmosphere of increasingly aggressive patriotism sparked by the war in Ukraine. Vitaly Milonov of "gay propaganda" fame recommenced that the Novorossiysk women be sentenced to "corrective labor," adding, "Next time, excuse me, some brainless she-goat will think twice."[4]

Rather than provoking outrage over content on the Internet, these videos were controversial for the dancers' use of public space. Their accusers insisted that the war monuments were sacred; indeed, police in Novorossiysk were purportedly considering charging them with "desecrating dead bodies and their places of internment." But others pointed out that the war memorials had long served the function of public parks, posting pictures of people swimming, tanning, and drinking at the Novorosiiysk memorial's beach. The problem was that the monuments' sites were never just one thing: they served a sacralizing function during particular rituals of memory (formal visits, anniversary commemorations) but were otherwise multipurpose public sites for most of the year. It is quite possible that the dancers did not think twice about their choice of backdrop, since it was simply a common public gathering place. But the moment the camera frames them in front of the memorial, the dance can start to look like a comment on the site itself. The critical viewer demands seriousness, but the dancers (and their supporters) saw only harmless fun.

Men at Twerk

In the middle of January 2018, freshmen cadets at an aviation academy in Ulyanovsk (a provincial town bearing Lenin's original last name) posted a clip inspired both by the Benny Benassi's 2002 "Satisfaction" and by a 2013 all-male British army parody, surely never intending to become the latest flashpoint in contemporary Russian culture wars.[5]

After the 2015 twerking scandals, the responses from the Russian officialdom were even more predictable. "It's a tragedy," declared famous aviator Magomed Tolboev. "It's a mockery. I would even compare it with Pussy Riot, when they made a mockery of the cathedral. And this is a cathedral of science."[6] The Rector of the

Ulyanovsk Aviation Institute, Sergei Krasnov, agreed. "This is a great insult to the Ulyanovsk region, and to veterans."

Calling a freshman dorm a "cathedral of science" only makes sense if you've never actually been to a freshman dorm. Indeed, critics were at great pains to construct a notion of the public sacred on the fly, as it were: the head of the Samara Flight Club called the clip "a scandal for aviation. Perhaps this would be forgivable by children, but not by people who are dedicating their lives to aviation."[7] Granted, this works in part because of the Stalin-era cult of aviators. But it is also part and parcel of the general official response to perceived cynicism. The answer to the question "Is nothing sacred?" has apparently become "Everything is sacred."

Sadly for the guardians of Russian public morality, this was not the end of the story. Soon people throughout the Russian Federation began posting their own "Satisfaction" clips, including construction students, agricultural students, emergency workers, stable jocks, a theater troupe, nurses, and, most delightfully, two headscarved and housedress-bedecked babushkas in a St. Petersburg communal apartment.[8]

After years of unrelenting Russian media attacks on the LGBT community (not to mention the ever-increasing rates of physical attacks for which the antigay campaign provides cover), what could be more heartening than apparently ordinary Russians showing solidarity with a group of boys who so comfortably inhabited a two-minute homoerotic performance? Could actual tolerance, or even acceptance, be in reach, somewhere over the rainbow?

Not exactly. It is true that some of the defenses of the Satisfaction boys have come in the face of anti-LGBT attacks. Certainly, Masha Gessen's story of the clip's condemnation by identically pantsuited sexologist sisters deserves a video campaign of its own.[9] A number of media commentators, both pro- and anti-Satisfaction, compare the performance to something one might see at the Moscow "Blue Oyster" bar, a gay nightspot whose name is both a gay pun in Russian and apparently inspired by a scene from the first *Police Academy* movie. Writing for the venerable extremist newspaper *Zavtra*, Roman Iliushchenko notes that the boys are obviously dressed in the uniform of "masochist f*ggots," before speculating a connection between the release of the video and Sergei Krasnov's cancellation of a contract with an American aviation company.[10] But most of the criticisms have less to do with the boys' supposed sexual orientation than their imperfect masculinity. One letter-writer to *Komsmolskaia Pravda* sees Satisfaction as the "natural result of the repression of men's masculinity," noting that the infamous, victim-eating serial killer Andrei Chikatilo was humiliated as a child by his mother's insistence on dressing him in women's stockings. In the Soviet 50s, listening to jazz records and wearing zoot suits was just a short step away from betraying the motherland; today, it seems that childhood cross-dressing and college-age twerking are the first steps on the road to cannibalism.

But the defense of the Satisfaction video is not waged on gendered grounds. Few bother to respond to attacks on the boys' masculinity, and virtually no one who defends them is arguing that the video is, indeed, "gay propaganda" (not that there's anything wrong with that). According to the logic of the pro-Satisfaction camp, the problem with the naysayers is not homophobia; the problem is that they are the enemies of fun. Indeed, the very title of the clip ("Satisfaction") would seem to reveal just what it is that its critics oppose: pleasure. What, the defenders ask, is wrong with playful, erotic dancing?

As Masha Gessen and others have already noted, the spirit animating the Satisfaction viral campaign and the online statements of support share an ethos with the 2012–13 protest movement, whose tactics often included expressing serious discontent in a clever, meme-worthy, and superficially nonserious manner. The Satisfaction supporters are definitely fighting for something, but it is not LGBT rights: they are fighting for the right to be frivolous. And, in an atmosphere of pompous, self-righteously serious political and cultural pronouncements by politicians and media figures, in an atmosphere that demands that the state and its officials be treated with the utmost seriousness, the right to be frivolous is no frivolous matter.

CHAPTER 8
PICTURES AT AN EXHIBITION

The Afterlife of High Art

Decoding memes requires that audiences know or learn a great deal of context but makes few demands when it comes to formal comprehension. Formally, most Internet memes resemble the older forms and legacy media that spawned them: image macro memes look like photographs, cartoons, or film stills, while viral videos look like, well, video. Memes are often made of "found" material—the cultural loadstars and detritus that can be made to mean something to a particular audience. When we compare memes from different cultural and linguistic milieux, it is both the context and the found material that will most obviously vary.

Russian meme-makers frequently use famous paintings as their starting point. According to Anastasia Denisova, this is "uncommon for Western meme makers and seems a local Russian peculiarity," noting that classic painting remixes have not been designated as a specific meme layout by prior scholars.[1] It would be an exaggeration to claim such remixes as particularly Russian; certain paintings, such as Da Vinci's *Mona Lisa*, Michelangelo's *The Creation of Adam*, or Munch's *The Scream*, have long been popular fodder for Internet humor. Where Russia does stand out is in what appears to be a broader range of paintings marshaled for memes, as well as a significant emphasis on classic Russian paintings.

That Russian meme-makers should look to Russian paintings is no surprise; the main reason this stands out is that these paintings are from the nineteenth century, a historical period from which very few Russian contributions are well-known outside of the former Russian imperial space. Ilya Repin's 1970–3 *Barge Haulers on the Volga* might well be the only one. In Russia, Repin himself is a household name, but it is one that would not mean much to nonspecialists in the United States and Western Europe.

Russian art becomes much more influential in the twentieth century, thanks to the contributions of the avant-garde in the century's first three decades. But these artists are underrepresented in Russian meme production. Kazimir Malevich and Marc Chagall, for instance, are almost invisible in the world of Russian Internet memes (though the 2020 protests in Belarus did lead to the replacement of the male figure holding a woman as they fly *Over Vitebsk* (1913) with a Belarusian policeman). Twentieth-century Russian visual culture is represented more through propaganda and movie posters, which formed a significant part of the mass culture of the time.

Instead of furnishing fodder for twenty-first-century Internet memes, the Russian art of the previous century is noteworthy for anticipating the Internet meme's form decades before the creation of the World Wide Web. Beginning the 1970s, the underground movement that called itself "Sots Art" parodied the conventions of the country's official socialist realist aesthetic and Soviet sloganeering through creative juxtaposition. Decades before Photoshop (and the Russian "fotozhaba"), the artistic team of Vitaly Komar and Alexander Melamid were inserting images of themselves as Young Pioneers (the Soviet equivalent of Boy Scouts and Girl Scouts) into classic paintings, Stalin's head into a variation on the classical theme of the biblical Judith beheading of Holofernes, and a recreation of the meeting at Yalta with E.T. replacing Roosevelt.

Russian postmodern art pointed the way for meme-makers to recycle art for their own purposes, but it was the nineteenth century that drew their attention. The Russian paintings that commonly recur in Internet memes (Repin's aforementioned *Barge Haulers* and *Ivan the Terrible Kills His Son*, Repin's *They Did Not Expect Him* [1886] and *Reply of the Zaporozhian Cossacks to Sultan Mehmed IV of the Ottoman Empire* [1890–1], Valentin Serov's *Girl with Peaches* [1887]) have the attraction of familiarity, easily comprehend realism, and clear emotional content.

They Did Not Expect Him is one of the most famous Russian paintings of the nineteenth century, and its endurance throughout

Soviet times is probably indebted to its subject matter: the sudden return from exile of a member of the revolutionary organization known as the People's Will. Though it portrays only one moment in time, it captures an entire story. While viewers first see the whole scene (the man who has just entered and the four people already in the room), they must look again slowly from one side to the other in order to decode all the action and reactions (the surprised and delighted surprise of the presumed wife and son, the confusion of the daughter, the shock of the old woman who may be the man's mother).

The painting has the perfect setup for a meme; it can be captioned, the man can be replaced by someone else, or the people already in the room can be swapped out for other figures. Or any combination of the above. Repin himself seemed to be aware of the flexibility of his chosen subject, since an earlier version of the painting has a young woman as the unexpected arrival.[2]

On the Internet, one version has Darth Maul shocking Yoda and other Star Wars characters, while another sets up a surprise confrontation between Darth Vader and Putin in an Imperial Stormtrooper costume. Zhdun naturally makes an appearance, as does a bodybuilder (posing for the assembled family), Moses brandishing the Ten Commandments, and the cast of *House*. There are also Repin crossovers, with the Barge Haulers coming through the door, much to the chagrin of the family. The meme is also useful for political statements, such as when the returning man is replaced by masked police officers with dogs, sometimes accompanied by the caption, "Too many repostings" (see Figure 4).

Barge Haulers on the Volga lends itself well to a particular type of political commentary, one that focuses on wealth inequality and miserable labor conditions. In one meme, the haulers are pulling an enormous cruise ship, with the caption, "Don't rock the boat, we'll spill the champagne" (see Figure 5). The implication is, of course, the opposite: the haulers have nothing to lose by rocking the boat, since they will never be the ones drinking the champagne. Or, as another meme puts it, "At least we have stability!" "Stability" is the watchword of the Putin era, always in contrast to the chaotic 1990s under Boris Yeltsin. A third meme makes the politics crystal clear. In the style of an

Figure 4 Repin's famous painting, *They Did Not Expect Him*, with masked police officers and a dog photoshopped in.

Figure 5 Repin's famous painting *Barge Haulers on the Volga* (The Volga Boatmen), now pulling a cruise ship. The caption: "Don't rock the boat, we'll spill the champagne!"

American editorial cartoon, the component parts of the painting are labeled. The Haulers are the "population of Russia," while the ship is full of "[parliamentary] deputies, bureaucrats, oligarchs." The caption: "Contemporary Russia in one picture."

The last Repin painting on our meme list is *Reply of the Zaporozhian Cossacks to Sultan Mehmed IV of the Ottoman Empire*. Both a festive and defiant scene, it depicts the Cossacks intemperate reply to a Turkish ultimatum, which starts with "Oh, Sultan, you Turkish Satan, brother and friend to the damn Devil and secretary to Lucifer himself," ends its second paragraph with "So fuck your mother" and continues in a similar vein for two more paragraphs.[3] One of the most famous paintings about Cossacks, it is, ironically, showing them engaged in the least Cossack-like behavior: writing, as opposed to looting and pillaging. But the drinks, smiles, and copious laughter convey a spirit of joyful aggression, even to viewers who might not be familiar with the letter's contents. As one of the Zaporozhian memes puts it, "Trolling: great fun since 1676."

What could be more perfect for the Internet age than a picture of rowdy men furiously writing an invective-laden response to something they have just read? Yes, the scene takes place in 1676, but the Zaporozhian Cossacks serve as a (very slow) precursor to a website's comments section—a 1676chan. A number of the resulting memes transpose the painting to a tech world context: "Dear Apple, we begin this letter"; "Tech Support writing a response to a disgruntled client"; "The whole department writes a letter to Websoft" (see Figure 6); "Zaporozhian Cossacks write translations for Google Translate." Others move the Cossacks to the world of Games Workshop's hugely popular Warhammer tabletop game's sprawling fictional universe, which includes a Slavic-derived world called "Vostroya." Hence the meme "Vostroyans write a letter to Games Workshop": "Hey! Moskals!

Figure 6 Repin's famous painting of Zaporozhian Cossacks writing a letter to the Turkish sultan, now repurposed as, "The whole department writes a letter to Websoft."

[an anti-Russian slur] Give us some new units for the tabletop game!" In another, the picture is actually from Warhammer art, but the caption is "The Vostroyans write to Abaddon the Despoiler (Warhammer's greatest Champion of Chaos Undivided)."

As much as the Zaprozhian memes lend themselves to jokes about the Internet, the painting is also tailor-made for political satire. True, plenty of Zaporozhian memes are devoid of political content. In one, the Cossacks are replaced by cats writing an email complaint to a famous Russian cat trainer; in another, all the figures are replaced by characters from the Simpsons (an inevitable permutation to virtually every painting-based meme); and in yet another, the Cossacks are responding to an ex-girlfriend who wants to get back together. But the moment reproduced by Repin was inherently political. Thus one of the memes seems to feature Donald Trump's cabinet.

The politics of the Zaporozhian memes are complicated, however, by the politics surrounding the Zaporozhians themselves. They were Ukrainian Cossacks, but their most famous portrayal in literature was by Nikolai Gogol, a Russophone Ukrainian writer who insisted that the Cossacks embodied a truly Russian spirit. Thus the Zaporozhian meme has become a particularly useful weapon for both sides of Russia's conflict with Ukraine. One of the Warhammer memes cited earlier starts in Russian but ends in Ukrainian. Another has Ukrainian prime minister Zelensky's cabinet dressed as clowns, writing a letter to Putin. In yet another, the Cossacks are laughing at the "Zevatniki" (a slur for Zelensky's supporters).

The Medieval Internet's Greatest Hits

It's the twenty-first century, and the Middle Ages are undergoing a renaissance. Thanks to the novel coronavirus, the year 2020 alone had all the hallmarks of medievalism, from a plague that kept the entire world indoors to the proliferation of outrageous conspiracy theories, not to mention the stores that, like the closed stacks of a monastic library, gave customers what they ordered without letting them inside. I write these words only a few hours after opening up a package containing a set of black facemasks with pictures of plague doctors and the slogan "Party like it's 1347."[4]

The new Middle Ages came a bit earlier to Russia, not only because of nostalgia for the days of Ivan the Terrible (with right-wing pundits calling for a return to the repressive ethos of his *oprichnina*) or the satire of that very nostalgia (Vladimir Sorokin's novel *Day of the Oprichnik*). Since 2014, the medieval period has inspired one of the biggest success stories of the Russian Internet, the phenomenon known as the "Suffering Middle Ages."

"Suffering Middle Ages" is the name of an online VKontakte community, a Facebook group, the entire category of memes based on medieval art and illustrations, a serious but a popular book about the historical period, and even a crowdfunded tabletop game. Based primarily on the often obscene marginalia found on the pages of medieval manuscripts, the people behind "Suffering Middle Ages" were not the first to draw attention to a phenomenon that looks so bizarre to modern eyes. Nor were they the only ones to post such images to the Internet. Technically, there is nothing about "Suffering Middle Ages" that could only have come from Russia; to the contrary, nearly all the images are from Western Europe. But the cleverness of the group's founders, the hilarity of their memes, and simple good luck turned medieval Europe into a Russian cottage industry.

"Suffering Middle Ages" dates back to 2014, hardly the days of yore by conventional measures, but on the Internet, a few years is like a lifetime. At the time, the group's founders, Konstantin Meftakhudinov and Iurii Saprykin, were second-year students at the Higher School of Economics in Moscow, where they attended a seminar led by noted medievalist Mikhail Boitsov.[5] At some point, Boitsov pointed to one of the images he was displaying and said, "Look at them. They're all suffering." Since the seminar itself was an intimidating experience, the students appreciated this rare opportunity to laugh along with their professor (Ovchinnikova). That night a group of friends starting swapping other "suffering" images, and they all began joking about the "Suffering Middle Ages" (Zhitkova). Originally they were just making memes and sharing them with friends, and it quickly took off, with glowing media coverage and celebrity subscribers and retweets from opposition leader Alexei Navalny. In 2019, the Russian edition of Forbes reported that the group had half a million subscribers on VKontakte and brought its founders a monthly revenue of up to 400,000 rubles (around $6,400 at the time). In addition to its merchandising, publishing, and gaming enterprises, "Suffering Middle Ages" is also on Facebook, significantly extending the community's reach beyond the confines of VKontakte.

Like the Repin memes from the previous chapter, "Suffering Middle Ages" depends on the repurposing of pre-Internet art for humor and commentary, but the similarities end there. Conventional art memes leverage ubiquity and familiarity (as with the *Mona Lisa*, Grant Wood's *American Gothic*, and Munch's *The Scream*), creating new meanings primarily through captions, photoshopping, or both. "Suffering Middle Ages" is premised on novelty and sheer weirdness. This does not mean that photoshopping doesn't happen; it does, though primarily with specific medieval images that have become recognizable thanks to the group's success. One image in particular, of a man naked from the waist down displaying his oversized scrotum for all to see, has become the group's symbol, if not its mascot. Nicknamed "Kolya," he is successfully photoshopped into any number of contexts (see Figure 7).

Figure 7 Kolya, the mascot for the Suffering Middle Ages group, with the strategically placed words "Sign here."

But, Kolya, like his scrotum, is exceptional. Most of the "Suffering Middle Ages" memes use an obscene, scatological, or peculiarly expressive medieval image and put words in the characters' mouths (through word balloons) or give the picture a contemporary spin. This is a technique that should be familiar to fans of Anglo-American memes that repurpose familiar film stills or panels from comics (such as the ubiquitous "Batman slaps Robin" and "Tony Stark rolling his eyes" memes). The comic book panels are perhaps the closest analogy to the Suffering Middle Ages memes, because the ones that are usually selected look cheesy or campy to contemporary eyes.

At the risk of explaining the patently obvious, we should note the meme-makers' primary strategy for finding the hilarity in bizarre, obscene, or puzzling medieval marginalia: making the characters talk as though they were our contemporaries. At the dinner table, six different men are eating, talking, or both, but now they are each accompanied by lines of dialogue: "I'm a vegan"; "No gluten for me"; "This is definitely lactose-free?"; "I'm fasting"; "G-d commanded us to keep kosher"; "Is this organic?" Meanwhile, the put-upon waiter says, "Lord, I've had it up to here with all of you!" (see Figure 8). In another, a woman appears to be pulling a dragon by a rope, while one man pokes it with a staff and another has been swallowed by the monster nearly whole (his legs dangle out of its mouth). The woman says, "Just

Figure 8 At a medieval feast. "I'm a vegan"; "No gluten for me"; "This is definitely lactose-free?"; "I'm fasting"; "G-d commanded us to keep kosher"; "Is this organic?" Waiter: "Lord, I've had it up to here with all of you!"

Figure 9 Dragon slaying reinterpreted: "Just a little bit more, Rover! The doctor just needs to take a look at your throat!"

a little bit more, Rover! The doctor just needs to take a look at your throat!" (see Figure 9).

A drawing of a woman with horns, bat wings growing from her arms, enormous breasts, and lets that look like fish tails now has the heading, "Comrade Director, let's make up our minds. Am I a mermaid, Batman, or Hellboy?" The carving of a man who looks like he's fellating himself is captioned "He 'liked' his own post." As two men saw through the genitalia of another man hung from his feet, one says, "I saw a great show last night, it's called *The Miracle Workers*." The other responds, "Good advice, I'll take a look after work." At the scene of a pitched battle, one knight in armor has his hand up against his ear. In the meme, he is saying, "Yes, dear, I can't talk right now. Put my beer in the fridge! What do you mean, I never do anything? I'm fighting!"

"Suffering Middle Ages" benefited from excellent timing. HBO's *Game of Thrones* (GoT) was only halfway through its run when the group first appeared, putting pseudo-medieval imagery in the public eye. Naturally, a number of the memes are GoT-themed, including a faux-medieval fan drawing of Arya killing the Night King, who is exposing his genitals in Kolya's familiar exhibitionist posture (while Bran sits by watching from his wheelchair). In another, the original image of Kolya and his wife standing before the doctor now has the doctor saying, "You have no right to the Iron Throne." Kolya replies,

Figure 10 Madonna and child. The baby asks, "What year is it?" "1348, my son." "Why the fuck did you give birth to me at the height of the plague? So I could die?"

"Are you nuts? I'm the Mother of Dragons," to which his wife says, "Enough, John, let's go."

When the coronavirus outbreak began, the paintings and marginalia of "Suffering Middle Ages" naturally lent themselves to making memes about plagues. In one, a mother holds a perplexed-looking newborn baby who, in keeping with the style of the times, looks like a worm with an adult human head on it. The baby asks, "What year is it?" "1348, my son." "Why the fuck did you give birth to me at the height of the plague? So I could die?" (see Figure 10). Others reflected the now common experience of living life over Zoom. A painting of Jesus and the apostles in which the apostles' heads look like they are radiating out of Christ's mouth becomes "Videoconferencing with the team during self-isolation." Another, which either quickly made its way to the wider Internet world, or perhaps initially came from there, rearranges da Vinci's *Last Supper* so that Jesus is sitting alone at the banquet table, with the apostles each appearing in his own Zoom window above Christ's head.

As I write this (in October 2020), the pandemic shows no signs of abating. Fortunately, we have the Middle Ages to show us how to suffer.

CHAPTER 9
GOING VIRAL
THE MEMES OF COVID-19

Memes at a Social Distance

The original plan for this book did not include the novel coronavirus that causes Covid-19, but then again, neither did any other plan hatched before the pandemic began. Were this a different kind of book, Covid would not require any particular acknowledgment. Dostoevsky, for example, has not been changed much by the coronavirus, nor has the study of the causes and effects of the October Revolution of 1917. Internet memes, however, are the opposite of timeless: they are perfectly calibrated to respond to the news cycle and the cultural moment at the speed of broadband.

The rise of Covid Internet memes is a deeply ironic phenomenon. Despite the objections registered in this book's Introduction, the "viral" metaphor for Dawkins's memes quickly caught on, which means that the viral understanding of the meme has been the most successful "meme" meme. As for Internet memes, the "viral" metaphor is inescapable, part of their DNA (or, to be more metaphorically and virologically correct, RNA).[1] One of the preoccupations of this book has been the relationship between Internet memes and memes as a broader category, as well as the connection between Internet memetic culture and life off-line. We saw how memes moved back and forth from cars (bumper stickers) to the Internet, with automotive circulation both replicating and extending circulation online. Rather than perpetuating the fiction of the online and the off-line as entirely separate realms, this book has argued for complementarity.

Meanwhile, In Russia

The pandemic has strained this complementarity or perhaps redefined it. With lockdowns, social distancing, and the redefinition of in-person contact as a public health threat, living online has much more clearly taken shape as a substitute for life off-line. As most of us try our best not to be viral vectors in real life, we spend an increasing amount of time spreading viral content over social media.

The coronavirus has challenged the customary relationship between "reality" (the biological and physical facts on the ground) and representation or simulation (the way we talk about reality). On the one hand, the virus is the revenge of the real: unliving strings of RNA do not care what we think about them and are largely resistant to our beliefs and prejudices. On the other hand, those of us who are lucky enough not to fall ill (or watch our loved ones get sick) experience the virus secondhand, through its representation. Internet memes use our representations of the real virus to create an unreal (memetic) virus that is safe to share. All the things the virus doesn't care about—what we think about it—are the stuff that coronavirus Internet memes are made of.

Activating Memory

In trying to understand, let alone prepare for, the pandemic, people in Europe, Russia, and the United States were at a luxurious disadvantage: there was nothing in their recent memory to draw on. By way of contrast, China had been through the 2002 SARS epidemic, while West Africa had coped with periodic outbreaks of Ebola.

Instead, the West had fiction: countless novels, movies, and television shows about apocalyptic pandemics ranging from plausible hemorrhagic viruses to variations on the theme of a zombie apocalypse. Though these stories certainly reached Russia, the country was a relative newcomer in producing them. As it happened, a television miniseries adapting Yana Wagner's 2011 killer flu novel *To the Lake* (*Vongozero*) under the generic title *Epidemic* had just premiered in November of 2019, concluding at the beginning of 2020.[2]

All the same, Russian Internet memes were more likely to turn to the country's history than to apocalyptic entertainment for inspiration. Russians in the West took to comparing the coronavirus restrictions to the Soviet lives they fled.[3] The panic-buying in the early days of the pandemic brought back memories of Soviet shortages and hoarding. As in the West, Russians created meme after meme about buying up toilet paper, but the resonance for the post-Soviet space was different. In the USSR, toilet paper was often quite difficult to find, rendering it a commodity that always had to be hoarded no matter what was going on in the country.

There is just one problem, though: given the digital divide between young people and pensioners (not to mention the various younger Boomers and Gen X-ers in-between), it is highly unlikely that the people who made coronavirus memes had a great deal of direct Soviet experience to draw upon. By 2020, the USSR had been gone for twenty-nine years. For the young people in Russia's meme world, the Soviet experience may have been more familiar than the "suffering" Middle Ages, but it was still another world.

For the younger generations, the touchstone for hardship is post-Soviet: the 1990s. The "Wild 90s" were difficult for the majority of the population, thanks to the impoverishment of the country and the rise in criminality. For many Russians online, the specter of a pandemic-related economic collapse translated visually into images of the 1990s.

The connection to the 1990s naturally lent itself to Internet memes. One of the most popular films of the 1990s, *Brother 2* (which technically came out in 2000 but is very much a part of the previous decade's culture) ends with the hero and a Russian prostitute sitting down in an airplane heading from Chicago to Moscow. When the flight attendant refuses to serve them vodka before takeoff, the prostitute takes off her wig, revealing a bald head, and says the now famous line, "Boy, you don't understand. We're flying home," prompting the attendant to serve them immediately. During lockdown, that image was now accompanied by the words, "Boy, you don't understand. Bring us an antiseptic. We're not flying anywhere."

The most productive 1990s meme was part of an international wave of related Internet memes responding to a series of fake news stories about the resurgence of wildlife now that people are staying home: "Nature is healing, we are the virus," as velociraptors return to the streets of Lisbon, a giant rubber duck floats under a drawbridge on the Thames, Godzilla comes back to Tokyo, and Geralt the Witcher fights monsters in Poland. One popular Russian response: "30 days of quarantine in Italy: the dolphins are back. 30 days of quarantine in Wales: the wild goats are back. 30 days of quarantine in Russia: the 90s are back" (accompanied by a still from one of a popular miniseries about 1990s-era gang wars).

The 1990s weren't the only historical period subject to this kind of memetic treatment. One meme uses the same three-part pattern and ends with a picture of armored men on horseback, while another shows a map of the USSR. But these memes were not backed up by the same sort of online chatter as the ones in which the Nineties were returning. As the most recent example of a Russian "Time of Troubles," the Nineties were all too easy to imagine, particularly since Putin and United Russia have continually used the "return of the Nineties" as the only (terrifying) alternative to the system currently in place.

Thus even as the hoarding behavior seen throughout the world in the early days of Covid would seem ready-made for a Soviet memetic makeover, the panic-buying of consumer goods simply sparked a variety of humorous visual representations of the goods in question. Indeed, toilet paper, as in the West (even though gastrointestinal distress was never high on the list of Covid symptoms), but also one commodity that probably would not even make a Western shopper's top 100 list of items to hoard: buckwheat groats (*grechka*). A typical Russian breakfast still includes a hot cereal or porridge (*kasha*), with buckwheat being one of the most common varieties. (It is also used in recipes for other meals.) Early to store, relatively nonperishable, buckwheat groats appear to be high on Russian's lists of practical emergency foodstuffs.

At the same time, there is nothing more ordinary or banal than buckwheat, so the frantic search for it can appear laughable, as can its invocation in an apocalyptic context. One meme shows a man dressed head-to-toe in hazmat gear, complete with gasmask, saying, "Let's go get some buckwheat groats." Another shows the iconic image from the last scene of *Fight Club*, with the protagonist and Marla holding hands as they start out of floor-to-ceiling windows, watching three office buildings explode. One building is labeled "coronavirus," another, "My plans for the year," and the third, "The ruble exchange rate." The chair to their left is labeled "working remotely," and a large bin to the right "buckwheat." Yet another meme is simply the picture of a moth, with the words, "Hi, alarmist! I'm Alevtina the moth. I've come for your buckwheat!"

Despite whatever the Covid denialists might say, the coronavirus is an undeniable human tragedy; millions have been infected, and over a million have died as of November 2020. Millions have lost their jobs and fallen into poverty, and the global economy is circling the drain. For the study of memes, however, it is a unique opportunity: the entire world is experiencing a phenomenon that spreads, if not at the speed of the Internet, with a rapidity that begins to converge with the way we assimilate and share information. Not only that it is a phenomenon whose grip on the world's attention is near universal. Memes that are created in one language are quickly translated and adapted into another, making it even more difficult than usual to determine their origins. This is where the common meme templates and macros become particularly important: a "Carl" meme riffing on the coronavirus can't spread across borders unless people around the world already know about Carl and his father.

Russia's meme world is in real-time cooperation with meme cultures around the globe, with Russian memes and viral videos attracting the attention of non-Russian-language media. As always, an element of the bizarre certainly helps. One stand-out element in Russian viral coronavirus content is the role of elderly women.

For nearly twenty years, an activist in the southern city of Krasnodar named Marat Dinaev has mobilized female senior citizens in support of Putin and his policies. A 2002 *Komsmolskaia Pravda* report called his group "*beshenye babki*" ("crazy grandmas" or "crazy old broads").[4] In 2013, his group garnered national attention again, this time under its official name, "The Putin Squads" (*otriady Putina*). The Putin Squads frequently hold protests and public events but are particularly effective as counterprotesters. Not only have "babushki" long occupied the role of casual moral authorities and street scolds; no one wants to be caught on camera in an altercation with an old woman. Though frequently derided as "brainwashed" and "mad," these elderly women leverage their perceived frailty to render themselves virtually bulletproof. The Ministry of Justice formally disbanded them in 2018, but that has yet to slow them down.[5]

In March of 2020, The Putin Squads released a video about the coronavirus on their YouTube channel; a month later, Roskomnadzor made them take it down, but it was too late: the clip had already spread across the world.[6] It showed three elderly women holding pictures of the virus cell; the one in the center (her hair hennaed to a red not seen in nature) declared that the virus was a fraud perpetrated on the world by Donald Trump to bring up the value of the dollar. One by one, they consign the pictures to a fire they've lit in a trash can, declaring the world and the country "cleansed."

It was an odd display, at once rejecting the reality of the pandemic while also engaging in a homemade ritual of sympathetic magic to rid the country of a problem that they claimed it did not have. That same month, another group of female retirees released a video in which they waved papers around in circles (3 to the left, 3 to the right, then a figure 8) to ward off the virus and protect the country. By the end of the video, they are joined by a man who looks like he might be Marat Dinaev himself, though he seems to be mocking them.

While elderly activists were hawking magical cures, intellectuals turned to literature for inspiration. Just as, after 9/11, the English-speaking world could not stop sharing W. H. Auden's poem "September 1, 1939," Russians during the early days of the lockdown found solace in a widely shared poem by Russian Nobel laureate Joseph Brodsky. Sharing a title with its first line, "Don't Leave Your Room" was written in 1970s as a critique of Soviet intellectuals who, rather than actively fight injustice, stayed home and griped. The line was used for graffiti in St. Petersburg (Brodsky's home city) not long after the pandemic hit Russia and went viral on the Internet soon after.[7] By the end of May, the majority of Russians surveyed recognized the line and could identify its author.[8]

In April, one of the most popular animated cartoons on the Russian Internet, Oleg Kuvaev's *Masiania* (2001–present), addressed not only the coronavirus but the Brodsky poem.[9] Masiana explains to her family that they're never going outside again, because outside is "violence, disease, politics, filth, viruses, rudeness, thievery, and other shit. There's nothing good out there." She adds, "Yeah, by the way, this is Brodsky. He's going to stay on our couch for a while."[10]

Grundel, her husband, is appalled: "What? What Brodsky? What the hell! No one asked me!" Meanwhile, Brodsky intones, "Don't leave the room, don't make the mistake and run" to which Grundel responds, "Shut up, Bro!"

Brodsky continues to chant his poem at inopportune moments, and, a year later, when they finally take a look outside before deciding to stay in longer, Brodsky is at it again: "Lock up and let the armoire keep chronos, cosmos, eros, race, and virus from getting in the door." Masyanya hits him: "You get the heck out of here, bro. You were to blame from the very beginning. Beat it, Bro!"

The clip is typical Masyanya—playful, eclectic, irreverent, and eminently meme-worthy.[11] It not only finds humor in the claustrophobia and tedium of lockdown but also draws attention to the communal nature of the experience of the "isolation" that gives this episode its name. Alone (or nearly alone) in our rooms, we are all consuming the same streaming entertainment, playing the same games, and seeing the same memes. The long-dead Brodsky telling us not to leave our rooms has colonized the computers (and therefore, the apartments) of an unknowable number of Russian Internet users. And, as with most viral content, if we are encountering it once, we will probably be encountering it again. No one asked for the Brodsky poem, but everyone received it, again and again, an odd, uninvited couch guest, inevitably finding itself the target of the simmering irritation of quarantine.

Why Won't Natasha Get Out of Bed?

In December 2019, when Covid-19 was just in the process of being identified in Wuhan, a new set of Russian memes was in its nascent stage. It took off before the virus spread to Europe, but in hindsight, it would look as though it were tailor-made for the pandemic. Initially featuring the face of a young woman ("Natasha") lying under the covers as her cats look down at her, when the meme caught on, it took on its now recognizable form. From then on, Natasha would be invisible; or, to put it more precisely, the viewer of the meme would be Natasha. Nearly all the memes are from Natasha's point of view, with four cats in a circle looking down on her (i.e., on us), while she is lying in bed.

While it might seem like a minor detail, this change in perspective is highly significant. The screen through which we receive audiovisual information has always been more than a mere display, but it takes a particular kind of formal playfulness to make the viewer more conscious of the screen's mediating role. Television has done this trick repeatedly over its decades-long history. The American living room as depicted on TV always had one major difference from its real-life counterpart: if it had a TV, we never saw it. Norman Lear's *All in the Family* (1971–9) repeatedly emphasized that the invisible TV televised living room functioned as the proverbial fourth wall. Archie and Edith would sit down in their chairs, turn on the television, and then look directly at the camera as if they were watching us watching them. The Natasha meme would now play a similar game with its audience. Never mind that most of us are not named Natasha; the cats are addressing us directly.

The classic Natasha meme starts with the line, "Natash, are you asleep?"[12] The others chime in: "It's already 6 in the morning, Natash.""Get up, we've knocked everything over." "Honestly, Natash, we knocked it all over." The situation is entirely domestic, but it is endlessly applicable to a whole variety of scenarios: something bad happened while you were sleeping, and now you're supposed to get up and take care of it. Or maybe just go back to bed.

Even worse, the night Natasha spent sleeping could stand in for her entire life, and all the opportunities she's missing, or all the dangers she's ignoring. In one meme, the cats tell her to get up because her biological clock is ticking. In another, they helpfully remind her, "Melanoma doesn't sleep, Natash." In still another, her problems began long before she was born: "Who are we descended from?" "From lions, of course." "And Natasha?" "From apes!" "Lord, how humiliating . . ." Inevitably, after the memes prolifcrate, they become self-referential. In one such meme, the implied viewer is no longer Natasha, but the meme-maker himself: "Get up, you moron!" "It's time to come up with new Natasha material." "You've got no girl, no cash—just your stupid memes." "Come on, at least clean our litterbox—we've shat all over it."

The combination of free-floating anxiety, a reluctance to wake up and face the world, and the coincidence of the meme's rise right before the pandemic made it perfect for the lockdown era. In one meme, the cats tell Natasha that the stores are out of toilet paper, the cats have unraveled the last roll, and even the newspapers are sold out. In another, they tell Natasha to wake up—everyone's wearing masks, so she should start sewing masks for the cats. The cats are panicking, and they refuse to chase any mice if they don't get face coverings. In yet another, they tell Natasha to wake up, because people are saying they'll have to stay home for an entire month, until May 1—what will they eat? They're running out of buckwheat. "What's going to happen to Easter, and to the festive shish-kebab?"

That particular month was the height of lockdown restrictions in Moscow; on March 30, the mayor issued a decree forbidding residents from leaving their homes, unless it was for emergency medical care, shopping at the nearest grocery or drug store, taking out the trash, or walking pets within a 100-meter radius of their homes.[13] On April 11, he instituted a system of digital passes for driving or taking public transportation.[14] One response was this Natasha meme: "Citizen, wake up!" "We had to taser you" "Where is your QR code?" "Why did you go beyond the 101-meter limit?" "That's a million-ruble fine."

As in the rest of the world, the coronavirus interfered with a number of long-range plans by the country's government. Putin was putting a new constitution on the ballot, one whose amendments would effectively allow him to stay in power until 2036 (the year he turns eighty-four). Despite Covid-19, the referendum went ahead in late June (it passed, in case anyone was wondering). Naturally, the Natasha meme was there to respond, all this time, the Russian words imply a generic male addressee: "Russian (Rossianin), get up" "We adopted it all." "The constitution." "The amendments, autocracy." "Get up, you need to pretend you voted." "Cocaine." "Russian, we basically adapted EVERYTHING. Honest!" The reference to cocaine is a pun, since the verb "to adopt" (as legislation) is also the word for "to take" (a drug). Perhaps the cocaine explains how the cats stayed awake while the Russian was asleep.

The Natasha meme became so widespread that it could remain recognizable even if all the cats were replaced with entirely different figures. The syntax of the meme (i.e., the arrangement of the images and the dialogue) proved to be more important than the felines who started the whole process. In one, the familiar house cats are replaced by lions. ("Natasha." "Because of this self-isolation." "we've gone a bit wild.") In another, they are replaced by politicians and public figures, starting with Putin and ending with the patriarch of the Russian Orthodox Church, all looking straight at us: "Get up, Natash!" "We've knocked over the whole economy" "The only hope is the fines" "And God, Natasha, and God . . ."

With the Natasha meme functioning more as a template than a set of specific images, it inevitably recombined with other meme templates. Even Carl from *The Walking Dead* got involved: "Carl, our time has passed!" "Do you know what they're saying instead of "Carl," now? Natash!" "Natash, Carl, Natash!"[15] One Natasha meme has all the cats replaced by different pictures of ALF (the 1980s alien puppet TV character), asking if she is sure that all the cats are really gone.

Still, the Natasha meme that best sums up the mood during the lockdown is one that went back to bases. All four cats are looking down at us, but this time they are saying, "Natash, are you asleep?" "Lie in bed awhile longer, Natash" "Don't get up" "Stay at home, we've locked everything up" "Just don't go out at all"

Joseph Brodsky could not have put it better himself.

Putin and the Pechenegs

By this point, we should not be surprised that Vladimir Putin makes a series of appearances in the memes of Covid-19. On March 24, 2020, after weeks of suspiciously low official rates of infection, Putin made a "spontaneous" visit to a Moscow communicable disease hospital to inspect the situation on the ground. He donned a yellow hazmat suite, complete with breathing apparatus, an event captured in photographs and video. Compared to certain other world leaders who refused to even put on a cloth face covering, Putin was demonstrating real prudence. But the optics were eminently meme-worthy.

The yellow-suited Putin was subsequently pictured as delivering food on a Moscow street, cooking meth with the stars of *Breaking Bad*, and dancing with the Teletubbies over the hills and far away. But perhaps the most politically pointed version of this meme simply used one of the most ubiquitous of Putin stock photos: the one that shows two guards opening up gilded doors in the Kremlin as the president confidently strides through. The meme replaces that familiar image of Putin with the president in the yellow hazmat suit, completely undermining the message of power and authority that the original photo so strongly projects.

Just two weeks later, the Russian president set off what *The Moscow Times* called a "meme storm" in an April 9 headline:

> Everything passes and this will pass. Our country has gone through many serious challenges: When tormented by the Pechenegs and the Polovtsians Russia has handled them all. We will defeat this coronavirus contagion.[16]

It was an odd variation on a familiar patriotic trope. The government and media have long invoked the suffering of the Second World War to rally the population against an enemy, which makes sense not only because the experience was so horrific, but because, in historical terms, Second World War was a recent event. Had Putin wanted to go back a bit further, there was no shortage of candidates, such as the Napoleonic invasion. These are hardly recent, but the country's school history and literature programs have etched this particular trauma into the national consciousness.

But the Pechenegs and the Polovstians? The Pechenegs fought the ancestors of the Russians, Ukrainians, and Belarusians for over two centuries, against Prince Igor in 920 and in the Battle of Kiev in 1036. True, the Polovtsians are more recent foes—they also battled Igor, but later waged war against Kievan Rus in the Battle of Kalka River in 1223. Unlike Westerners, Russians can probably be counted on to recognize these names, but, as enemies go, the Pechenegs and the Polovtsians are not exactly the Legion of Doom.

This does not mean that most Russians know a great deal about either group; meme-makers imagine an uptick in Internet searches about them. One meme draws two Pechenegs, with one asking, "So, are we trending on Google yet?" The other answers, "No, it's the Polovtsians" (see Figure 11).

At a moment when the country needed reassurance, Putin's military-infused bluster came off as laughable. Framing every threat in terms of foreign invasion is the weapon of choice in the Russian state media's arsenal, but this particular historical comparison only highlighted just how exposed and unprepared Russia's leadership was. What real lessons could medieval warfare provide twenty-first-century epidemiology? Donald Trump was widely ridiculed for advising Americans to drink bleach to combat the coronavirus; Putin was stopping just short of suggesting Russians sacrifice a goat.

Naturally, Twitter raked him over the coals. A user posting under the name "Denis the Alien" (Denis Chuzhoi) writes:

Figure 11 Pechenegs on the Internet: "So, are we trending on Google yet?"; "No, it's the Polovtsians."

Me: I hope Putin will stop constantly reminding us about the
Great Patriotic War [the Second World War] and will find
something else for Russia to be proud of.
Putin: Pechenegs.[17]

Meme-makers immediately seized on the phonetic resemblance
between "Pecheneg" and "pechen'e" ("cookie"), as well as between
"Polovtsy." "Plov" ("pilaf") and various Russian words involving
swimming. In one meme, the Pecehengs are represented by a
gingerbread man; in another, a Twitter user offers up Pechenegs and
Polovotsy, with pictures of cookies and swimmers (see Figure 12).

These visual puns also make sense because of the strangeness of
the two group's names. It would be entirely possible for an educated
Russian to spend their entire adult life without ever saying "Pecheneg"
aloud. Or it would have been, had it not been for Putin's comment.
By alluding to a thousand-year-old battle, Putin had inadvertently
summoned the Pechenegs back, but this time for the purposes of jokes
rather than bloodletting.

The crossover between the Pecheneg memes and the Natasha
memes was a foregone conclusion. Now the cats tell Natasha to wake
up because "We've been tormented by Polovtsy." "And Pechenegs,
Natash." "And the coronavirus infection, honest." In another, the cats

Figure 12 A tweet exploiting the phonetic similarities between "cookies"
and "Pechengs" and "Polovtsians" and "swimmers": "Have some Pechenegs!
And have some Polovtsians."

complain that the Pechenegs ("And the Polovtsians, Natash") have taken all their money. Other memes place a heavier emphasis on the medieval nature of the threat: "There are Pechenegs everywhere, Natash." "They've made a raid." "They're demanding tribute." "Get up, quickly, put on your armor." "Grab a shield" "Then we'll chase off the Polovtsians and the coronavirus." In another, the cats tell Natasha not to bother to get up. They beat the Pechenegs. And they beat the Polovtsians. "But with the coronavirus it all got completely fucked."

Finally, we have a meme where the cats are replaced by drawings of medieval barbarians: "Natash, get up!" "They beat us all, Natasha" "They beat the Polovstians and the Pechenegs, honest." "Get up, Natash, there's a lot of work to do." "We have to gather tribute and redo the sidewalks." "And there are people to impale, Natash." This meme is inspired: in all the rhetoric about fighting off the barbarians, couldn't someone think of it from their point of view? The line about the sidewalks is a reference to the Moscow mayor's insistence on continuing his urban beautification plan, and virus be damned. In one Natasha meme, we have the virus, the desire for a return to normalcy, discontent with top-down plans of what "normal" should look like, and even a (probably unintentional) reference to the labor market. The Pechenegs might be odious, but we could really use them for underpaid labor. Like the Central Asian migrants many Muscovites love to hate, but who play an important role in the economy, imaginary enemies like the Pechenegs are an indispensable element in Putinist rhetoric.

Art and Isolation

The crown jewel of Russian coronavirus memes is a project whose ingenuity and playfulness captivated the attention of a sensation-starved world: the Facebook challenge called "Izoizoliatsiia." A portmanteau of the Russian for "isolation" and an abbreviation for "visual arts," Izoizoliatsiia had the particular advantage of being entirely wordless.

It started out as a game between Katerina Brudnaia-Cheliadinova and her husband, Dmitri Dologrukov, a way to fill the tedium of lockdown, inspired by other online groups such as "covidclassics" on Instagram and "Sfotkai tipa Rembrandt" ("Take a Rembrandt-Style Photo") on Facebook. First, he put on a hat and a painted beard to pose as Van Gogh's 1887 *Self-Portrait with Straw Hat*. By the end of March, Burdnaia-Cheliadinova set up a Facebook group.[18] By the time *The New York Times* got whiff of the phenomenon for its April 25 story, the group had more than 540,000 members with a flood of new images every day.[19]

The Izoizoliatsiia rules constitute the sort of game familiar to anyone who has followed the various "challenges" that have spread across the Internet (with the "Icebucket Challenge" being among the most famous). Participants recreate a painting or poster using only the materials they have at hand. But one of the rules makes Izoizoliatsiia stand out: no Photoshop allowed. Unlike so many of the memes we have seen in this book, these are not "fotozhabas." The process for creating the image is analog and low-tech, but the result is a digital image to be shared far and wide. The only way these memes could be more hand-made is if they were assembled pixel by pixel.

The results are hilarious: surrealist masterpieces reproduced with food from the refrigerator, household objects taking the place of angels. They are a testament to the ingenuity of countless people stuck home with nothing to do, as well as the apotheosis of the Russian Internet's tendency to invoke the classics of Western and Russian art in meme creation.

But they are more than that. The Izoizoliatsiia are the moment when the off-line and the online come together. Who would care if they were just another set of photoshopped memes? Despite the fact that they are all based on preexisting images, the Izoizoliatsiia memes have something that was rare in the age of mechanical reproduction and virtually nonexistent with the rise of digital technology: the aura of the original, the real. The group's very name stresses the loneliness and atomization brought on by pandemic restrictions, but the images they have produced are a small, homeopathic remedy for isolation. Yes, we are all at home, but we can transform the stuff of our isolation into something communal, something shared. We cannot go outside, but we can sneak out as memes.

CONCLUSION
THE QUICK AND THE DANK

Coming to a firm conclusion about Russian Internet memes is a self-defeating task, given the speed at which memes develop (and the relatively glacial pace of traditional publishing). Timeliness is the flip side of obsolescence, and I am painfully aware that, to the extent that this book is a snapshot of Russian MemeWorld circa 2020, it could look quaint or nostalgic within just a few years. More to the point, the preoccupations of Russian memes, as well as their patterns of circulation, could be completely different. Most of the memes themselves will almost certainly cease to be current. As many of my readers no doubt know, an overused or played-out meme is sometimes called a "dank meme," although the phrase "dank meme" is so overused that the word "dank" might itself be considered irredeemably dank. This is a vortex of irony from which few can emerge unscathed.

If the trends and features I have identified continue, then the value of discussing them is clear. If they do not, then this book will have contributed to the understanding of a particular historical moment. I can live with that. Eventually, the most dated aspect of this book will be the assumption that Internet memes themselves might seem novel.

Yet the time we spent analyzing particular memes and trends was also in the service of larger points, one about Russia and the other about memes in general.

Regarding Russia: the creativity and wit demonstrated by so many of these memes complicate any attempt to portray Putin-era culture as solely the story of increasing, top-down control of the media. Even in the face of restrictive legislation, the Russian meme community has flourished. Meme makers and consumers show their independence not just through expressing outright opposition to state policies and propaganda but also by not always taking the state seriously. The more that Russian officials and the state media try to impose a narrative of patriotism, "traditional values," and solemnity, the more apolitical irreverence proves itself political. No wonder the media was briefly outraged over twerking videos; it's hard to feel like you're being taken seriously when the Internet is shaking its collective ass in your direction.

Regarding memes: the story starts with Dawkins's *The Selfish Gene*, develops into the fringe "science" of memetics, and truly takes off when the term "meme" is applied to a set of viral phenomena on the Internet. In other words, memes started as an off-line concept before really catching on as a component of cyberspace. But the examples of Russian car culture (dashcams and bumpers stickers) remind us that once memes "moved" to the Internet, they never stopped circulating outside of it. The rise of the Internet meme helps us recognize memes when they are off the Internet as well. We do not need to wait for the rise of truly effective and integrated wearable computing to see that the line between online and off-line has become more difficult to distinguish. Being "always online" does not mean ceasing to exist off-line; rather, it means a hybrid state of being that might be invisible to some who grew up without the Internet and distasteful to others.

In *Another Roadside Attraction*, novelist Tom Robbins wrote, tongue in cheek, that "human beings were invented by water as a device for transporting itself from one place to another."[1] Hardcore memeticists such as Susan Blackmore posited that human consciousness is a meme-generated illusion, implying that people serve as vehicles for the dissemination of memes.[2] I am not proposing anything nearly so radical as either Robbins' or Blackmore's denial of human agency; rather, that observing the ways in which memes spread from people to the Internet to objects can suggest one possible way of understanding the human "always online" experience. We are thinking beings who presumably have agency, but we are also nodes in a complex system for the circulation of memes.

NOTES

Acknowledgments

1   Recordings of the lectures are available on the Jordan Center YouTube
    Channel (https://www.youtube.com/playlist?list=PL52nR9X22dlMtCO1
    MvjZcN6FLsfPIecFa) and on eliotborenstein.net

Introduction

1   The Chrysler Building meme is probably the result of confusion about
    New York City landmarks. Ivan is clutching the top of the building while
    biplanes buzz around him, a clear allusion to the original *King Kong*
    movie. Kong, however, climbed the Empire State Building.

2   An English translation of the play can be found in Laurence Senelick's
    Russian Satirical Comedy: Six Plays (New York: Performing Arts Journal
    Publications, 1983). In Russian, Gaidai's film is known as *Ivan the
    Terrible Changes His Profession*; in English it is sometimes called *Ivan
    Vasilievich: Back to the Future.*

3   Derived from "LOL" ("Laugh out loud"), the phrase "for the lulz" is used
    to explain the reason behind silly behavior and is often the justification
    for the antics of an Internet troll.

4   Three years later, an intoxicated visitor to the Tretyakov attacked the
    painting with a metal pole.

5   Scholarship on the Russian Internet continues to grow, though primarily
    in the Russian language. In English, Eugene Gorny's *A Creative History
    of the Russian Internet* (Riga: VDM Verlag, 2009) is a good place to start.
    Andrei Loshchack's *InterNET: A History of the Russian Internet* (https://
    www.youtube.com/playlist?list=PLFRQplrTcKj_d20omBf8dpWwd3qonfl
    2H) documentary series on YouTube is both informative and fascinating,
    while the online journal *Digital Icons: Studies in Russian, Eurasian, and
    Central European New Media* provides a wealth of information. Readers
    of Russian might also want to look at Aleksei Krivopal's *Runet: Novoe*

sosvezedie v galaktke internet (Ridero, 2017) and Sergei Kuznetsov's *Oshchupyvaia slona: Zametki po istorii russkogo Interneta* (Moscow: NLO, 2011).

6 The Russian Federation (RF) is a multiethnic, multilingual country with many residents who speak Russian as a second language. The dominant language for the Internet in the RF is nonetheless Russian, and I regret that I do not have the linguistic competence to include online activity in any of the other languages commonly spoken on Russian territory.

7 Anastasia Denisova, *Internet Memes and Society: Social, Cultural, and Political Contexts* (New York: Routledge, 2019). See, for example, the work of Andrew Chapman and Bradley E. Wiggins, "Crimea River: Directionality in Memes from the Russia-Ukraine Conflict," *International Journal of Communication* 10 (2016): 451–585, as well as portions of his book *The Discursive Power of Memes in Digital Culture: Ideology, Semiotics and Intertextuality* (New York: Routledge, 2019).

8 Robert Coalson, "Russia's Dangerous Struggle With Obscurantism," Radio Free Europe/ Radio Liberty, October 3, 2013. https://www.rferl.org/a/russia-repin-art-orthodoxy/25125740.html

9 See my 2008 book, *Overkill: Sex and Violence in Contemporary Russian Popular Culture.*

Chapter 1

1 "Go God Go," *South* Park Season 10 Episode 12 (November 1, 2006) and "Go God Go XII" *South* Park Season 10 Episode 13 (November 8, 2006).

2 Richard Dawkins, *The Selfish Meme: 40th Anniversary Edition* (Oxford: Oxford University Press, 2016), 328.

3 Dawkins, *The Selfish Meme*, 251.

4 Borenstein, "Survival of the Catchiest: Memes and Postmodernism in Russia," *Slavic and East European Journal* 48.3 (2004): 462–84.

5 Charles J. Lumsden and E. O. Wilson, "Translation of Epigenetic Rules of Individual Behavior into Ethnographic Patterns," *Proceedings of the National Academy of Sciences of the USA* 77 (1980): 4382.

6 It also travels poorly to other languages, containing two liquid consonants ("l" and "r"), which trip up a wide range of non-English speakers, and right before two affricates ("ch" and "g") that can also be challenging. Compared to "culturegen," meme is like "Kodak," the brand name designed specifically to be viable across multiple languages.

7   See, for example, Scott Atran, "The Trouble with Memes: Inference versus Imitation in Cultural Evolution," *Human Nature* 12 (2001): 351–81 and "The Revealed Poverty of the Gene-Meme Analogy: Why Memetics Per Se Has Failed to Produce Substantive Results," *Journal of Memetics* 9 (2005). http://jom-ermt.cfpm.org/2005/vol9/edmonds_b.html

8   David L. Hull, "Taking Memetics Seriously: Memetics Will Be What We Make It," in Robert Aunger (ed.), *Darwinizing Culture* (Oxford: Oxford University Press, 2001), 47–8.

9   The spread of email in the 1990s was also the process of getting users to realize that they did not need to print out everything that was on their screen in order for it to be "real," "official," or subject to preservation.

10 Mike Godwin, "Meme, Counter Meme," *Wired,* October 1994. https://www.wired.com/1994/10/godwin-if-2/

11 Richard Brodie, *Virus of the Mind: The New Science of the Meme.* Reissued edition (Carlsbad: Hay House, 2011).

12 Henry Jenkins, Sam Ford, and Joshua Green (eds.), *Spreadable Media: Creating Value and Meaning in a Networked Culture* (New York: New York University Press, 2013).

Chapter 2

1   This is not to say that his enthusiasm was untempered. In a late poem, he wrote that "agitprop" (agitational propaganda) "sticks in my craw," and lamented "stomping on the throat of his own song."

2   See Catriona Kelly, "'A Laboratory for the Manufacture of Proletarian Writers': The *Stengazeta* (Wall Newspaper), *Kul'turnost',* and the Language of Politics in the Early Soviet Period," *Europe-Asia Studies* 54.4 (2002): 573–602 and Birgitt Breck Pristed, "Soviet Wall Newspapers: Social(ist) Medan and an Analog Age." Pristed makes the connection between the *stengazeta* and later digital media.

3   On Soviet jokes, see Emil Draitser, *Taking Penguins to the Movies: Ethnic Humor in Russia* (Detroit: Wayne State University Press, 1998); Seth Graham, *Resonant Dissonance: The Russian Joke in Cultural Context* (Evanston: Northwestern University Press, 2009); Jonathan Waterlow, *It's Only a Joke, Comrade! Humor, Trust and Everyday Life under Stalin (1928-1941)* (Oxford: CreateSpace 2018).

Notes

4   Timothy O'Keefe and Keneth G. Sheinkopf, "Advertising in the Soviet
     Union: Growth of a New Media Industry," *Journalism and Mass
     Communication Quarterly* 53.1 (Spring 1976): 80–7.

5   This claim is made on the website for Retro Soviet Ads, but I have not
     found any external confirmation of this fact.

6   https://www.retrosovietads.com/

7   See Eliot Borenstein, "Public Offerings: MMM and the Marketing of
     Melodrama," in Adele Barker (ed.), *Consuming Russia* (Durham: Duke
     University Press, 1999), 49–75.

Chapter 3

1   Andropov and Chernenko each had very short terms in power and are
     rarely represented in Russian memes.

2   Yurchak argues that the idea of Lenin's physical resurrection was never
     a significant part of the discourse around Lenin's embalmed body
     (Alekei Yurchak, "Bodies of Lenin: The Hidden Science of Communist
     Sovereignty," *Representations* 129.1 (2015): 145.

3   Aleksey Yurchak. "The Canon and the Mushroom: Lenin, Sacredness, and
     Soviet Collapse," *HAU: Journal of Ethnographic Theory* 7.2 (2017): 165–98.

4   Stephanie Sandler, "Sex, Death and Nation in the *Strolls with Pushkin*
     Controversy," *Slavic Review* 51.2 (1992): 294–308.

5   Daniil Kharms, *Today I Wrote Nothing: The Selected Writings of Daniil
     Kharms,* edited and translated by Matvei Yankelevich (New York: Harry
     N. Abrams, 2009).

6   Anna Akhmatova, *Smuglyi otrok brodil po alleiam (1911).* Sobranie
     sochienii. Tom 4 (Moscow: Ellis Lak, 2000), 8–9.

7   It would only be in 2006 that *Under the Sky of My Africa: Alexander
     Pushkin and Blackness* would be published by Northwestern University
     Press. It was the first extended study of the topic. Catherine Theimer
     Nepomnyashchy, Nicole Svobodny, and Ludmila A. Trigos (eds.), *Under
     the Sky of My Africa: Alexander Pushkin and Blackness* (Evanston:
     Northwestern University Press, 2006).

Chapter 4

1   https://www.youtube.com/watch?v=hYijpOjCYYw

2   Walker's spoken English is thoroughly American. His Russian
     pronunciation and intonation sound authentic, and he speaks in

complex sentences with a rich vocabulary, though he does occasionally mix up his grammatical genders.

3   In 1997, the Duma adopted the Law on Freedom of Conscience and Religious Associations, which granted Judaism, Islam, Buddhism, and the Russian Orthodox Church official recognition, as well as giving a lesser status to a number of other faiths and establishing a registration regime for new religious movements. Nine years later, the rules on registration were tightened, as were the restrictions on any religions movement that was not one of the main four. See Zoe Knox, "Religious Freedom in Russia: The Putin Years," in Mark D. Steinberg and Catherine R. Wanner (eds.), *Religion, Morality, and Community in Post-Soviet Societies* (Bloomington: Indiana University Press, 2008).

4   Walker and his wife homeschool their children, which is highly unusual in the Russian Federation. It fits their "traditional values" image but also could easily be used to make them seem freakish or fanatical if the media were not so well-disposed toward the Jolly Milkman.

5   Walker claims that his actual statements about "Italian mozzarella" were taken out of context to make them seem political. "At some point in the middle of the interview, I joked that 'there won't be any of that Italian cheese of yours, ha ha ha'—it was filmed, uploaded, and went viral as an American supporting import substitution. I was like, 'What are you gonna do?'" Even here, his words are open to interpretation: "What are you gonna do?" most likely refers to his attitude about the market in the age of sanctions but could just as easily refer to his inability to control the viral video phenomenon that frames him in a particular light (Narina Georgian, "'Ne budet vashego italianskogo syra. Akhakha.' 'Veselyi molochnik Dzhastas Ualker razoblochil mem pro sebia.'" Prospect mira March 10, no year given. https://prmira.ru/news/ne-bude t-vashego-italyanskogo-syira-ahaha-veselyij-molochnik-dzhastas-uo lker-razoblachil-mem-pro-seb/

6   See Elliott Oring, *Joking Asides: The Theory, Analysis, and Aesthetics of Humor* (Logan: Utah State University Press, 2016); Raúl Pérez, "Racist Humor: Then and Now," *Sociology Compass* 10.10 (2016): 928–38; Leon Rappoport, *Punchlines: The Case for Racial, Ethnic, and Gender Humor* (Westport: Prager, 2005).

7   Linor Shifman, *Memes in Digital Culture* (Boston, MA: MIT Press, 2013); Wiggins, *The Discursive Power of Memes in Digital Culture.*

8   https://www.youtube.com/watch?v=IiI3N6Qd_hU

9   The subject of the video uses feminine pronouns, verb forms, and adjectives to describe herself.

Notes

10 https://www.youtube.com/watch?v=vmTOmjjgNEw

11 https://www.youtube.com/watch?v=1gY88V8kbHM

12 https://vk.com/candybober

13 https://www.youtube.com/watch?v=vmTOmjjgNEw

14 https://www.youtube.com/watch?v=komPusxme18&ab_channel=Skull Chanell

15 https://www.youtube.com/watch?v=etQiMtjs_6I

16 https://www.youtube.com/watch?v=24XBX0Wkmpw&ab_channel= MerleBlanc

17 Iurii Snegirev, "Bednaia Sveta. Kak zatravili 'nashistku' iz Ivanova," *Rossiiskaia gazeta,* February 16, 2012. http://rg.ru/2012/02/16/sveta .html

18 http://lurkmore.to/%D0%9F%D0%BE%D1%80%D0%BE%D1%81% D1%91%D0%BD%D0%BE%D0%BA_%D0%9F%D1%91%D1%82%D1 %80. English-language translation is the author's own.

19 Anna Karpova, "Sozdatel' 'Vatnika' Anton Chadskii: Kak ia stal russofobom," *Snob,* October 14, 2014. https://snob.ru/selected/entry /82278/

20 Anton Chadksii, "Vatnik i nenavist," *rufabula,* January 6, 2015. https:// rufabula.com/author/anton-chadsky/264. English-language translation is the author's own.

21 Though not the subject of the *entire* book, English-language memes about Putin are among the many sources examined in Alison Rowley's clever and insightful *Putin Kitsch in America* (Montreal: McGill, 2019).

22 Vadim Elistratov, "Karl: kak populiarny mem iz seriala 'Khodiachie mertvetzy' dobralsia do Rossii I vyshel v oflain," *TJ,* April 22, 2015. https://tjournal.ru/internet/54838-coral

23 Kira Iarmysh, Tweet, April 22, 2015. https://tjournal.ru/internet/54838 -coral. Navalny's facility with pop culture memes runs in the family. At the end of the joint trial of Navalny and his brother, Oleg, on trumped-up embezzlement charges, cited the film *Guardians of the Galaxy:* "There's this phrase [used by one of the characters]: 'I am Groot.' That phrase has more meaning and explains my crime more than anything that has been said her in the past few months" (Natal'ia Dzhanpoladova, "A ne nado bylo na Putina lezt," *Radio Svoboda,* December 19, 2014. https://www.svoboda.org/a/26753111.html

24 "The Resurrection of Stoned Fox; British Artist's Badly-Stuffed Creation Enjoys a Second Life as a Russian Internet Celebrity," *The Daily Mail,*

March 11, 2013. https://www.dailymail.co.uk/news/article-2291620/M
eet-Stoned-Fox-The-badly-stuffed-creature-reborn-Russian-internet
-celebrity.html

25 Kristie McCrum, "Welsh Artist's Stuffed eBay Fox Becomes Russian
    Internet Sensation," *WalesOnline*, March 13, 2013. https://www.walesonl
    ine.co.uk/news/local-news/welsh-artists-stuffed-ebay-fox-2013129

26 "Interview with Adele Morse, Creator of Stoner Fox," *Crappy Taxidermy*,
    June 30, 2014. https://crappytaxidermy.com/post/90420823835/inter
    view-with-adele-morse-creator-of-stoner-fox

27 "Potavchenko prosit zapretit' dizain-vystavku 'Uporotyi lis,'" *Izvestiia*,
    March 20, 2013. https://iz.ru/news/547100

28 "Rospotrebnadazor proverit kafe, gde zhdut 'Uporotogo lisa,'" *bbc.com*,
    April 2, 2013. https://www.bbc.com/russian/society/2013/04/130402
    _stoned_fox_cafe

29 Pavel Lobkov, "Uporotyi lis: 'Ia ne poluchu 5-komnatnuiu kvartiru v
    Groznom I rosskiiskii passport,'" *TV-Rain*, April 20, 2013. https://tv
    rain.ru/teleshow/here_and_now/uporotyj_lis_ja_ne_poluchu_5_k
    omnatnuju_kvartiru_v_groznom_i_rossijskij_pasport-341621/. The
    Stoned Fox is yet another memetic controversy in which Alexei Navalny
    became embroiled. In 2014, he wrote a tweet mocking Municipal
    Deputy Aleksei Lisovenko. In addition to calling Lisovenko a "drug
    addict," he likened the deputy's signature "Sincerely yours, Lis" to the
    Stoned Fox (the Russian for fox being "Lis"). Andrei Kozenko, "Izdrevle
    letchik i uporotyi lis. Ocherednoi sud nad Alekseem Naval'nym
    poluchilsia sovsem uzh absurdnym," *Znak.com*, April 18, 2014. https://
    www.znak.com/2014-04-19/sud_po_obvineniyu_alekseya_navalnogo
    _v_klevete_vyshel_sovershenno_absurdnym

30 Sof'ia Vertoporokh, "Uporotyi lis kak 'Chernyi kvadrat,'" *Fontanka.ru*,
    April 8, 2013. https://www.fontanka.ru/2013/04/08/048/

31 Georgii Pankratov, "Iskusstvo uporotykh lis," *Vzlgiad*, March 29, 2013.
    https://vz.ru/opinions/2013/3/29/626543.html

32 Regina Konstantinova, "Dutch Hospital's Cute Monster Sparks
    Unexpected Furor in Russia," *Sputnik*, February 10, 2017. https://sputnik
    news.com/art_living/201702101050553707-zhdun-sculpture-meme/

33 Alena Radchenko, "V Rade poiavilsia 'Zhdun,'" *Pravda.com*, February
    24, 2017. https://www.pravda.com.ua/rus/news/2017/02/24/7136340/

34 "V 'Mezhigor'e' ustanovili skul'pturu Zhduna," *Gordon*, June 7, 2017.
    https://gordonua.com/news/society/v-mezhigore-ustanovili-skulpturu
    -zhduna-191928.html

Notes

35 Dmitrii Travin, "Ne tol'ko russkii zhdnun," *Vedomosti*, March 8, 2017. https://www.vedomosti.ru/opinion/articles/2017/03/09/680395-ne-to lko-russkii

Chapter 5

1 This is known as the "Streisand effect." When Barbara Streisand tried to curtail the publication of photos of her Malibu home online, she only drew attention to them. The attempt to suppress publicity only leads to more publicity.

2 Mar Krutov, "Skazochnyi sud. 30 tysiach za fotografiiu nadpisi 'Putin—*****'," *Radio Svoboda*, May 14, 2019. https://www.svoboda.org /a/29940562.html; "Nadpis' 'Putin pidor' v Iaroslavle: otkryto delo o vandalizme," *Grani.ru*. https://grani-ru-org.appspot.com/Politics/Russia /President/m.276302.html

3 Artemy Troitsky connects to the song "Speedy Gonzales" as performed by Pat Boone. This is supported by the numerous "Путин—хуйло" comments on YouTube videos of the song. After listening to Boone's performance (which five decades later is even more appallingly racist than one might imagine), I determined that the main thing the two songs have in common is the immortal words "la la la" (but not the melody).

4 "Putin Huylo (remix by AstrogentA)," *YouTube*, April 21, 2014. https:// www.youtube.com/watch?v=-n2D4giJDyU; "Pesnia 'Putin, hello' gruppy 'Teleri' vzorvala Internet (video)," *Podrobnosti*, May 6, 2014. https:// www.youtube.com/watch?v=-n2D4giJDyU; "V efire ukrainskogo kanal ispolnili znamenity khit o Putine," May 29, 2014. http://ivona.bigmir. net/showbiz/stars/393110-V-efire-ukrainskogo-kanala-ispolnili-zna menityj-hit-o-Putine; zOlena Goncharova, "Kharkiv, with New Russian Song, Becomes Capital of Anti-Putin Music (VIDEO)," *Kyiv Post*, July 11, 2014. https://www.kyivpost.com/article/guide/music/lifestyle-blog-soccer-fans-chant-putin-khuilo-makes-it-to-world-fame-353315.html

5 Lina Klymenko. "The Language of Party Programmes and Billboards: The Example of the 2104 Parliamentary Election Campaign in Ukraine," in Ruth Wodack and Bernhard Forchtner (eds.), *The Routledge Handbook of Language and Politics* (New York: Routledge, 2017), 450–1.

6 The phrase's enduring legacy has been ensured somewhere between he constellations Cygnus and Lyra. In July, Ukrainian astronomers gave star TYC 3541-945-1 the official designation "Putin- Huilo!" (Polly

Mosendz, "Adopted Star Dubbed 'Putin Is a D**khead' Will Not Be Renamed," *The Atlantic*, July 7, 2014. https://www.theatlantic.com/in ternational/archive/2014/07/adopted-star-dubbed-putin-is-a-dkhead -will-not-be-renamed/374039/).

7   Vladimir Sorokin, *Goluboe salo* (Moscow: Ad Marginem, 1999).

8   Vladimir Sorokin, *Day of the Oprichinik*, Translated by Jamey Gambrell (New York: FSG, 2011), 169–71.

9   See Valerie Sperling, *Sex, Politics, and Putin: Political Legitimacy in Russia* (Oxford: Oxford University Press, 2014) and Tatiana Mikhailova, "His Family and Other Animals: Putin's Soft Power," in Helena Goscilo (ed.), *Putin as Celebrity and Cultural Icon* (London: Routledge, 2012), 65–81.

10 See "Communism Is Soviet Power + Electrification of the Whole Country," *Seventeen Moments in Soviety History*. http://soviethistory .msu.edu/1921-2/electrification-campaign/communism-is-soviet-power -electrification-of-the-whole-country/./

11 See the entry for "Chmo" in *Vikislovar'*. https://ru.wiktionary.org/ wiki/чмо.

12 "Russian Propaganda Edits Out Racist Comment about Obama," *The Moscow Times*, November 22, 2016. https://www.themoscowtimes.com /2016/11/22/russian-propaganda-edits-out-racist-comment-about-oba ma-a56254

13 In English this term is usually reserved for Internet-facilitated gatherings that take place in real life.

14 "Mikhail Zadornov – Obam CHMO," *YouTube*, January 21, 2015. https ://www.youtube.com/watch?v=pSL-oxX4UwU&ab_channel=%D0%AE %D0%BC%D0%BE%D1%80FM

15 Less than three weeks after the American presidential election, "Biden Is a Schmoe" was spotted on a Russian car. Michele A. Berdy. https://tw itter.com/MicheleBerdy/status/1331161243646914561

16 "Transcript: Greta Thunberg's Speech at the U.N. Climate Action Summit," *National Public Radio*, September 23, 2019. https://www.npr .org/2019/09/23/763452863/transcript-greta-thunbergs-speech-at-the-u -n-climate-action-summit

17 Tony Wesolowsky, "The Russian Bear Is Spooked by Greta the Eco-Activist," *RFE-RL*, October 3, 2019. https://www.rferl.org/a/russia-greta -global-warming/30197495.html

18 Alexei Naval'ny, "Vse nenavidiat Gretu Tunberg," *YouTube*, September 26, 2019. https://www.youtube.com/watch?v=8EjjPsxd

Xqk&ab_channel=%D0%9D%D0%BE%D0%B2%D0%BE%D1%81
%D1%82%D0%B8%D0%A0%D0%BE%D1%81%D1%81%D0%B8
%D0%B8

19 Iuliia Latynina, "Pionerka Greta Tunberg," *Novaia gazeta*, September
26, 2019. https://novayagazeta.ru/articles/2019/09/26/82123-pionerka-g
reta-tunberg

20 Yuliya Minkova, *Making Martyrs: The Language of Sacrifice in Russian
Culture from Stalin to Putin* (Rochester: University of Rochester Press,
2018: 36).

21 See Catriona Kelly, *Comrade Pavlik: The Rise and Fall of a Soviet Boy
Hero* (London: Granta Books, 2005).

22 Even Reeves himself has got in on the act. In a comic book cowritten
with Matt Kindt, he made sure that one panel features the character
modeled on him in the "Sad Keanu" pose. Josh Grossberg, "Keanu
Reeves New Comic *BRZRKR* Puts a Spin on 'Sad Keanu' Meme," *Syfwire*,
September 1, 2020. https://www.syfy.com/syfywire/keanu-reeves-comic
-brzrkr-sad-keanu-meme

23 For a fascinating discussion of the cult of Elon Musk and the "'Take
That, Elon Musk" memes, see Fiona Bell and Ekaterina Olson
Shipyatsky two-part "A Spectre Is Haunting Russia, or A Chilling
Journey from Ulyanovsk to Silicon Valley," *All the Russias*, October
13 and 14, 2020. https://jordanrussiacenter.org/news/a-spectre-is-haunti
ng-russia-or-a-chilling-journey-from-ulyanovsk-to-silicon-valley-part-
i/#.X8P9TBNKjvU and https://jordanrussiacenter.org/news/a-spectre
-is-haunting-russia-or-a-chilling-journey-from-ulyanovsk-to-silicon-va
lley-part-ii/#.X8P9UBNKjvU

24 Andrey Loshak, *Internyet: A History of the Russian Internet*. *Current
Time*. https://en.currenttime.tv/p/7345.html/. The journalist's name is
usually, and more properly, transliterated as "Andrei Loshchack," but
this page uses a different spelling.

25 "Shuvalov otvetil na Maska slovami 'russkii narod bolee talantliv," *RBK*,
February 7, 2018. https://www.rbc.ru/society/07/02/2018/5a7ab7d89a79
47170c793dee

26 For more on the connection between the Soviet space program and the
campaign against religion, see Victoria Smolkin, *A Sacred Space Is Never
Empty: A History of Soviet Atheism* (Princeton: Princeton University
Press, 2018), 84–105.

27 Peter Graff, "Russian Lawmakers Slam 'Armageddon' Film," *Reuters*,
October 9, 1998.

Chapter 6

1 The original upload (http://www.youtube.com/watch?v=oavMtUWDB TM) had reached nearly eighteen million hits as of February 10, 2014. This does not include the numerous reposts and "sing-along" versions, with millions of views of their own.

2 For a fascinating examination of Russian memes on Buzzfeed, see James Rann, "Meanwhile in Russia: Buzfeed, Russia, and the West," *The Calvert Journal*, November 19, 2013. https://www.calvertjournal.com/ articles/show/1776/buzzfeed-russia-virals

3 Lily Rothman, "In Soviet Russia, the Oscars Host You," *Time*, February 22, 2015. https://time.com/3715747/bob-hope-russian-reversal/

4 https://knowyourmeme.com/memes/meanwhile-in

5 "Why Almost Everyone in Russia Has a Dash cam," *Wired*, February 15, 2013. https://www.wired.com/2013/02/russian-dash-cams/

6 Bryan Dugan, "Why So Many Russian Drivers Have Dashboard Cams," *Mental Floss,* September 3, 2014. https://www.mentalfloss.com/article /48952/why-do-so-many-russian-drivers-have-dashboard-cams

7 John Stewart, "How I Meteored Your Motherland," *The Daily Show*, February 19, 2013. http://www.cc.com/video-clips/lstf5e/the-daily-show -with-jon-stewart-how-i-meteored-your-motherland

8 Keith Gessen, "Stuck," *The New Yorker*, August 2, 2010. https://www .newyorker.com/magazine/2010/08/02/stuck-3

9 As Robert Agenbright puts it, "these driver-citizens are emerging publics, people who are creating a civil society without specifically meaning to do so" ("Avtomobilshchina: Driven to the Brink in Moscow," *Urban Geography* 29.7 (2008): 683).

10 Stephen J. Collier, *Post-Soviet Social: Neoliberalism, Social Modernity, Biopolitics* (Princeton: Princeton University Press, 2011), 1–30.

11 Kseniia Knorre-Dmitrieva, "Speshish' v ad? Ustupliu dorogu," *Novaia gazeta*, March 4, 2016. https://www.pressreader.com/russia/novaya-gaz eta/20160304/281736973542150

12 Marina Galperina, "Why Russians Are Obsessed with Dash-Cams," *Jalopnik*, June 13, 2012. https://jalopnik.com/why-russians-are-obsessed -with-dash-cams-5918159

13 Using Google Trends, Kristiana Naydenova identifies August 2014 as the time when "Squatting Slav" became a popular search term, peaking in October 2017 ("Squatting Slavs: A Culture, a Stereotype,

or Just a Meme?"*Diggit Magazine*, August 11, 2018. https://www.dig gitmagazine.com/articles/squatting-slavs-culture-stereotype-or-just -meme).

14   Any connection to the Russian-derived Jewish surname "Gopnik" remains a mystery.

15   As a force on the Russian street, the gopniki had significantly receded by the late 1990s. See Hilary Pilkington (with Elena Starkova), "'Progressives' and 'Normals,'" in Hilary Pilkington, Elena Omel'chenko, Moya Flynn, Ul'iana Bliudina, and Elena Starkova (eds.), *Looking West? Cultural Globalization and Russian Youth Cultures* (State Collage: Pennsylvania University Press, 2002), 125.

16   Hilary Pilkington describes the "gopnik strategy" as "territorial defense and attack." (*Russia's Youth and Its Cultures: A Nation's Constructors and Constructed* (New York: Routledge, 2013), 300).

17   The main characters of "Real Guys" never refer to themselves as gopniki, but their clothes, vocabulary, and bearing are undeniable evidence that the term fits. Moreover, the rich characters in their orbit routinely refer to them as "gopniki," although usually out of earshot. For a more thorough discussion of the show, see Irina Souch, *Popular Tropes of Identity in Contemporary Russian Television and Film* (London: Bloomsbury, 2019), Chapter 5.

Chapter 7

1   Though it might seem like a dated example, *Footloose* is actually a perennial. It was a hit musical on Broadway starting in 1998 (with a tenth anniversary touring revival in 2008), while the 2011 film remake was a box office success.

2   For just one popular example, see *Despicable Me* (2010).

3   The head of the dance studio complained that the video was posted without the permission of the girls, their parents, or the school (Anna Dolgov, "Russian Girls Twerking in 'Patriotic' Costumes Cause Outrage," *The Moscow Times*, April 14, 2015. https://www.themosco wtimes.com/2015/04/14/russian-girls-twerking-in-patriotic-costumes -cause-outrage-a45725).

4   Alec Luhn, "Three Jailed in Russia for Dance Video Filmed at Novorossiysk War Memorial," *The Guardian*, April 26, 2015. https://ww

w.theguardian.com/world/2015/apr/26/three-jailed-in-russia-dance-video-novorossiysk

5   "Flight Students of the Institute in Russia Benny Benassi 'Satisfaction,'" *YouTube*, January 16, 2018. https://www.theguardian.com/world/2015/apr/26/three-jailed-in-russia-dance-video-novorossiysk; "British Army Soldiers Dancing to Satisfaction [Benni Benassy]," *YouTube*, August 25, 2015. https://www.youtube.com/watch?v=X_bQa2H1-Ck

6   Ivan Davydov, "Tantsui, poka molodoi, mal'chik," *Republic*, January 18, 2018. https://republic.ru/posts/89001

7   Dar'ia Chistoprudova, "Kursanty Ul'ianovskogo uchilischcha o svoem 'griaznom' tantse: 'Eto byl neobdumannyi detskii postupok," *Komsmol'skaia Pravda*, January 18, 2018. https://www.kp.ru/daily/26783/3817167/

8   "Russian Babushkas Embrace the 'Satisfaction Challenge,'" *Russia Beyond the Headlines,* January 22, 2018. https://www.rbth.com/lifestyle/327337-russian-babushkas-satisfaction-challenge

9   Masha Gessen, "How Russia's Hilarious, Homoerotic 'Satisfaction' Became a Nationwide Meme of Solidarity," *The New Yorker*, January 22, 2018, https://www.newyorker.com/news/our-columnists/how-russias-hilarious-homoerotic-satisfaction-became-a-nationwide-meme-of-solidarity

10 Roman Iliushchenko, "Molodye, smelye . . . i bezgolovye," *Zavtra*, January 23, 2018. https://zavtra.ru/blogs/molodie_smelie_i_bezgolovie

Chapter 8

1   Denisova, *Internet Memes and Society*, 100.

2   A. L. Kaganovich et al., *Zamechatel'nye polotna* (Leningrad: Khudozhnik RSFSR, 1961), 260.

3   There are numerous translations of this letter. I have chosen the most colloquial one I could find. Lenny Flank, "The Zaporozhian Cossack Letter," *Hidden from History*, February 16, 2017. https://lflank.wordpress.com/2017/02/16/the-zaporozhian-cossack-letter/

4   In keeping with the overall spirit of 2020, the masks turned out to be too uncomfortable to wear.

5   This Iurii Saprykin is sometimes referred to as "Saprykin the Younger," so as not to confuse him with his uncle, a well-known journalist and critic.

Chapter 9

1   Though viruses can contain RNA or DNA or both, coronaviruses are composed of RNA.

2   Broadcast of the series was temporarily suspended due to the government's unhappiness with the fifth episode, in which civilians are slaughtered as part of the state's quarantine measures.

3   See, for example, Jenny Craik, "How My Soviet Mom Prepared Me for the Coronavirus Pandemic," *The New Yorker*, April 22, 2020. https://www.newyorker.com/humor/daily-shouts/how-my-soviet-mom-prepared-me-for-the-coronavirus-pandemic

4   The phrase could also be translated as "tons of money," although that doesn't seem to be appropriate here. Timur Olevskii, "Kak ustroeny 'Otriady Putina': rasskazyvaet rukovoditel' 'beshenykh babok,' napavshikh na shtab Naval'nogo v Krasnodare," *Nastoiashchee vremia*, Jue 5, 2017. https://www.currenttime.tv/a/28598148.html

5   Alena Kazakova, "Skandal'nye 'Otriady Putina' likvidiroval Miniust, no sdavat'sia ne khotaiat," *MK*, November 22, 2018. https://www.mk.ru/social/2018/11/22/skandalnye-otryady-putina-likvidiroval-minyust-no-sdavatsya-oni-ne-khotyat.html

6   "Roskomnadzor prigrozil zhurnalistam strafom za rolik, gde pensionerki iz 'Otriadov Putina' szhigaiut koronavirus v vedre," *Novaia gazeta*, April 23, 2020. https://novayagazeta.ru/news/2020/04/23/160964-roskomnadzor-potreboval-ot-zhurnalistov-udalit-rolik-gde-pensionerki-iz-otryadov-putina-szhigayut-koronavirus-v-vedre

7   "Iosif Brodskii pomogaet rossianam borot'sia s koronavirusom," *Epigraf.info*, March 29, 2020. http://www.epigraph.info/lenta/43567-iosif-brodskij-pomogaet-rossiyanam-borotsya-s-koronavirusom.html

8   "Opros: bol'shinstvo rossian znaiut, komu prinadlezhit fraza 'Ne vykhodi iz komnaty,'" May 24, 2020. https://стопкоронавирус.рф/news/20200524-1200.html

9   Oleg Kuvaev, "Masiania, Epizod 142. Izoliatsiia," August 2, 2020. https://mult.ru/эпизод-142-изоляция/

10 Translated by The Russian Reader. "Masyanya in Isolation," *The Russian Reader*, April 14, 2020. https://therussianreader.com/2020/04/18/masyanya-in-isolation/

11 This was the 142nd episode. Over the years, Mayanya has spawned a wide range of catch phrases that have spread throughout the Internet.

12 In Russian, if a name ends in an "a," you can drop the "a" in informal speech but only as a form of address: "Natash, are you asleep?" but not "Natash is asleep."

13 "Moscow Orders Citywide Quarantine Starting March 30," *The Moscow Times*, March 29, 2020. https://www.themoscowtimes.com /2020/03/29/moscow-orders-citywide-quarantine-starting-march-30-a 69789

14 "Moscow Issues around 1 Million Digital Passes in First Day of System Operation," *Tass*, April 13, 2020. https://tass.com/society/1144123

15 The crossover went both ways. There is a Natasha meme where the cats are addressing Karl, explaining that there's a pandemic, and now Natasha is in fashion.

16 "Putin Sets Off Meme Storm by Comparing Medieval Invaders to Coronavirus Quarantine," *The Moscow Times*, April 9, 2020. https:// www.themoscowtimes.com/2020/04/09/putin-sets-off-meme-storm -by-comparing-medieval-invaders-to-coronavirus-quarantine-a6993 1. The translation of Putin's remarks in this article renders "Polovtsy" as "Cumans." This is an acceptable translation, but, given all the words play involve "Polovtsian," it is confusing. I have replaced "Cumans" with "Polovtsians" in this particular quote.

17 "'Vinovaty pechenegi.' Runet otreagiroval na obrashchenie Putina k nadody," *BBC*, April 8, 2020. https://www.bbc.com/russian/other-news -52221161

18 Liubabva Zaitseva, "Kak gruppa 'Izoizoliatsiia' stala khitom feisbuka v karantiinyi period," *Afisha*, April 9, 2020. https://daily.afisha.ru/infopo rn/15203-kak-gruppa-izoizolyaciya-stala-hitom-feysbuka-v-karantin nyy-period/

19 Anton Troianovski, "Bored Russians Post Silly Art Parodies: The World Has Joined In," *The New York Times,* April 25, 2020. https://ww w.nytimes.com/2020/04/25/world/europe/russia-Facebook-art-parodies.html

Conclusion

1 Tom Robbins, *Another Roadside Attraction* (New York: Batman, 2003), 12.

2 Susan Blackmore, *The Meme Machine* (Oxford: Oxford University Press, 200), Chapter 17, 219–34.

INDEX

Index

144

Index